Life-Writing for Victims of Childhood Maltreatment: The Write to Justice and Recovery

Heather B. Fox Griffith

July, 2014

September 30, 2014

ISBN 978-0-9937706-6-1

Abstract

Autoethnography as a qualitative research methodology produces data suitable for meta-analysis when the interest is in gaining insight into the lived experience of childhood victimization and the relevant cultural, social, historical and political context of individual experience. The life-story of childhood victimization as told in _The Write to Justice_ (Fox, 2014) is based on the personal experience of the researcher. The interdisciplinary meta-analysis of the text generates a mapping and creation of an inventory of social, political and cultural influences that create a terrain of contextual stressors that are likely causal to the subsequent violence, maltreatment and harm inflicted on the child who was conceived outside of marriage and born in the 1950s. The researcher/author provides a thick description of embodied experience and meaning making as an important part of the process of recovery and toward sensitizing the reader. This phenomenological approach to research methodology addresses concerns with researcher subjectivity and bias and agrees that subjective experience is grounded in self-experience (Anderson L., 2006). Nevertheless, autoethnography reaches beyond the subjective experience of _self_ to include the larger social world. Phenomenological research provides information that can be broadly applied to a population that has experienced the phenomenon of interest. A person who has experienced the phenomenon of interest, even when that person is the researcher self, is representative of that population and the experience can be applied to developing nomothetic or "generalized theoretical understandings" of social processes (Anderson, 2006, p. 385).

Keywords: childhood victimization, autoethnography, meaning-making, expressive life-writing, hermeneutics, recovery, healing

Table of Contents

1.   **Life-Writing for Victims of Childhood Maltreatment: The Write to Justice and Recovery 7**

BACKGROUND 8

RESEARCH QUESTION 10

RESEARCH INTERDISCIPLINARITY 11

AUTOETHNOGRAPHY META-ANALYSIS 12

2.   **Childhood Victimization 14**

UNDERSTANDING TRAUMA 18

MOTHERS AS OFFENDERS IN CHILD MALTREATMENT 26

3.   **Feminist and Postmodernist Perspectives on Gendered Violence 27**

WOMEN, VIOLENCE AND AGGRESSION 29

POSTPARTUM MENTAL DISORDER AND CHILD HARM 33

DIFFICULT KNOWLEDGE 42

4.   **Evocative Autoethnography 47**

THE PHENOMENOLOGY OF EXPERIENCE AND MEANING-MAKING 49

NARRATIVE EXPRESSION 52

THE INTERACTIVE PROCESS 55

DIGITAL STORYTELLING AND CONTEMPORARY MEDIA 56

5.   Creative Non-fiction 60

PERCEPTIONS OF TRUTH 62

DOES CHANGING THE STORY IN CREATIVE NON-FICTION MEAN WE HAVE CHANGED OUR PERCEPTION OF TRUTH? 64

PERSONAL MYTHOLOGY AND POETRY 67

6.   Victim Narratives and Therapeutic Justice 70

HISTORICAL JUSTIFICATION FOR INCLUSION OF VICTIM IMPACT STATEMENTS 70

THERAPEUTIC JURISPRUDENCE, RESTORATIVE JUSTICE AND VICTIM NARRATIVES 72

THE IMPACT OF CRIMINAL VICTIMIZATION ON VICTIMS 73

COMPASSION AND SOCIAL JUSTICE 74

7.   Research and Applied Ethics 78

PURPOSIVE WRITING 81

ETHICAL PROBLEMS WITH IDENTIFYING SUBJECTS 84

PRIVACY, CONFIDENTIALITY AND PROTECTION FROM HARM
87

8.   Healing and Recovery 89

RELIGION AND SPIRITUALITY INTEGRATED WITH THE
HEALING PROCESS 90

FORGIVENESS 93

EMPOWERING THE VOICES OF VICTIMS 95

CHALLENGES AND PROBLEMS 97

9.   Conclusion 100

References 105

1. Life-Writing for Victims of Childhood Maltreatment: The Write to Justice and Recovery

This interdisciplinary research generates a meta-analysis of a revised, self-published autoethnography, _The Write to Justice_ (Fox, 2014)[1] that describes and discloses the lived experience of childhood victimization and the subsequent journey toward healing and recovery. _The Write to Justice_ is a transmedia publication which includes a public domain website, a short video consistent with the genre of digital storytelling and a book in print and eBook formats (Fox, 2014). As qualitative research methodology, autoethnography integrates the _process_ of authoring with the creation of a _product_ that is based on the lived experience of the subject - the researcher _self_. Autoethnography expresses difficult knowledge in the context of relevant cultural and social factors understood through a reflective process. The meta-analysis of the data produced in _The Write to Justice_ evaluates the relevance of life-writing toward the development of nomothetic or generalized theoretical understanding of social processes that impact victims of childhood trauma and maltreatment. Moreover, this analysis

---

[1] The Write to Justice (2014) can be found at http://www.thewritetojustice.com

acknowledges the context of childhood victimization when the perpetrator of the maltreatment is a woman and the victim is female and explores the problem of internalized misogyny.

There are opportunities within the traditional and therapeutic justice systems that are intended to support victims through the process of disclosure and in describing the impact victimization has had on their lives. This paper explores how the current practice of victim disclosure through the Victim Impact Statement (VIS) fails to address problems associated with loss of voice, especially for childhood victims of maltreatment. The problems and benefits of creative non-fiction and factual writing are discussed.

Background

In telling difficult stories of childhood victimization often authors have to make decisions about what information will be disclosed, especially when we understand that 'my' story is not just my story, but also the story of others. The need to protect relational others from being identified in autoethnography must be balanced with the legitimate needs and rights of victims to name their alleged abusers and to navigate beyond shame and silence through disclosure. The factors that impact what decisions are made about identifying others can pose complex ethical issues that are not always easy to reconcile. Making a representation of serious claims such as childhood maltreatment requires a commitment to the

8

truthful and factual descriptions of events but there will always be a discretionary process that determines what is disclosed. In autoethnography, the researcher is engaged in the process of writing the *self* retrospectively. It is not the *actual self* that is written. Rather, the written *self* is a collective representation of actions, experiences, decisions, meanings, interpretations and descriptions, realized and imagined. Even when a writer is representing factual events as accurately as possible, the *self* of autoethnography is a description, a symbolic or metaphoric self. According to Bruner, "the distinction between narrative fiction and narrative truth is nowhere nearly as obvious as common sense and usage would have us believe" (1991, p. 13).

When research interest is directed toward understanding the lived experience of childhood victimization as a phenomenon, rather than on determining the guilt or innocence of an alleged abuser; if we are seeking to understand the impact of childhood victimization through the voices of adult survivors who write their experiences, the ethical decisions made about disclosure should always consider what is in the best interest of the victim, as well as relational others. Ellis suggests there are times when the best interests of others do not come ahead of the best interests of the subject and when, despite concerns of harm, factual disclosure must be made (2007, p. 24). Victims of childhood maltreatment have a right to give voice to our lived experiences and to tell our stories, even when this is troubling to others. Frank (2013) suggests that sharing recollected memories creates an important "moral opportunity to set right what was done wrong or incompletely" (Kindle Locations 2157-2158) in the past.

Research Question

Is creative non-fiction in autoethnography a productive qualitative research methodology for the study of the lived experience of childhood victimization, leading to a deeper understanding of this complex social problem? The question of productivity is assessed from an interdisciplinary perspective to determine how life writing can support healing and recovery for victims of childhood maltreatment. Can narrative expression through life-writing and creative non-fiction support the process of meaning making, resilience, recovery, and healing for childhood victims?

The subject of this paper is the autoethnography *The Write to Justice* (Fox, 2014), a story of childhood victimization written from the perspective of the survivor and researcher *self*. The ethical concerns encountered while writing with candour were reconciled through the process of writing expressively and through creative non-fiction. Etherington suggests there are important guidelines for writing and ethical decision-making (2004, p. 148). The question *"What is the impact of this work on me?"* is relevant to some of the ethical challenges faced by a writer when making decisions about revealing subject names, the identity of the researcher *self* and the

10

identities of relational others (p. 148). Etherington's question about self-impact should be followed by another, namely: *what is the impact of this work on others* and *is there a risk that ethical constraints on a researcher intended to protect the identity of the subject perpetuate a legacy of silence and protection of the alleged abuser.*

Research Interdisciplinarity

This proposal investigates life-writing for the purposes of disclosure and therapeutic expression of the experience of childhood victimization. Childhood victimization is a complex social problem that demands insight into the causal factors that are both individual and social. Moreover, in order to facilitate healing and recovery the researcher must integrate the knowledge and insights of several relevant disciplines and fields of study in order to find common ground and create new solutions to the problem of childhood victimization and recovery from it - solutions that can create important and constructive social change. No single discipline or field of study has the ability to adequately address this problem. This research integrates the knowledge and findings of original data, relevant literature, and the concepts, theories and insights contributed by selected disciplines and fields of study. These findings are applied to an analytic process to deepen our understanding and insight into the lived experience of childhood maltreatment and the value of transmedia expression and life-writing.

Contemporary interdisciplinarity includes research and stakeholders outside of universities who contribute significantly to the various bodies of research. This has been critical to the needs of victims. The Victim's Rights Movement of the 1970s led to calls for reform to the way victims were treated (Algonquin College, 2013). The Canadian Association for Prevention of Crime (CAPC) made 79 recommendations of its own by 1983, calling for an increase in the participation of victims in the justice process. The CAPC successfully argued for the inclusion of Victim Impact Statements at the time of sentencing of convicted offenders. The 1985 *UN Declaration on the Basic Principles of Justice for Victims of Crime and Abuses of Power* (United Nations General Assembly, 1985) attracted signatory countries from around the world. Eventually, the inclusion of Victim Impact Statements was codified into the Canadian criminal justice system in 1988, through s.735 of the Criminal Code (Algonquin College, 2013). Now, the most important stakeholders, the victims, contribute in a meaningful way to the body of knowledge and insights into the complex problem of childhood and other victimizations.

Autoethnography Meta-Analysis

Repko maintains that in order to generate a "more comprehensive understanding" (2011, p.3) of a complex problem there must first be a robust understanding of the interested disciplines and their concepts, assumptions, theories and insights. The process of meta-analysis applied to this research involves scrutiny of relevant conceptual and theoretical assumptions. The understanding generated by meta-analysis suggests new ways to interpret the data collected through autoethnography from an integrated, interdisciplinary perspective. An exploration of critical issues in Childhood Victimization and recovery will identify, define and describe the embodied, lived experience of childhood victimization; identify problems consistent with the consequences and sequelae to childhood victimization. Research can determine the dimensions of those problems by identifying dominant cultural and historical contributors to childhood victimization, as experienced by the victim. We must examine the ways our current models of justice address childhood maltreatment as well as evaluate the overall societal response to the problem. Understanding causality is important if we are to successfully investigate what steps are likely to be significant to a victim's ability to heal and recover. Specifically, this research is interested in identifying the benefits, problems and therapeutic value of life-writing and creative non-fiction for victims who disclose and express difficult knowledge.

2. Childhood Victimization

There are special concerns with the effects of trauma, maltreatment and crime on children, which are not well understood from a developmental perspective. David Finkelhor has made significant contributions to the theory of developmental Victimology (2008). According to Finkelhor, "victimization has enormous consequences for children, derailing normal and healthy development trajectories" (2008, p. 9). Finkelhor further claims there are a number of problems with the status of children that prevent many people from having a clear portrayal of the scope and nature of childhood victimization (2008). The maltreatment of children is not fully incorporated into crime statistics. Margolin and Gordis suggest there is no formal designation as crime victims for children who are victims of interparental violence (Margolin G., 2000). A child is in a state of change and development and the impact of maltreatment must be understood within the context of the child's status and abilities.

> From a developmental psychopathology perspective, the effects of violence can only be understood in the context of the changing child, and his or her changing environment, including the evolving familial and societal expectations for the child (Pynoos 1993). That is, the child's experience of violence is not only determined by the nature of the violent events but by the child's own capacities to appraise and understand violence, to

respond to and cope with danger, and to garner environmental resources that offer protection and support (Finkelhor &

Kendall-Tackett 1997). These responses are inextricably linked to the child's general cognitive, emotional, and physical capacities (Marans & Adelman 1997) (Margolin G., 2000, p. 450).

Despite the persistent belief that children are not traumatized by experiences they are unlikely to remember later in life, Margolin and Gordis (2000) assert that victimization can affect children even when it occurs in early infancy. Child maltreatment impacts personality formation and creates significant mental health consequences in children who are affected. The ability of a child to have positive social interactions with others can be highly disrupted and problematic. Academic performance is often impacted and victimized children are at a greater risk for becoming offenders themselves as sequelae to their own experiences (Margolin G., 2000).

There are obvious problems that limit the ability of the very young or dependent child or youth from disclosing maltreatment to others. Maltreatment of children and dependent youth is mostly perpetrated by known individuals and not strangers. When a child can disclose maltreatment by family members such as physical or emotional abuse, neglect and indirect abuse like witnessing violence against other family members, the complaint will likely be responded to by social agencies other than police. Self-advocacy is another important issue when it comes to how the maltreatment of children and youth is understood and responded to socially and in law. Adults have the ability to speak on their own behalf and to express their experiences and needs. Children do not have the same capabilities due to age and their dependency on caregivers. There are developmental limits that can impact communication skills, create dependency problems that increase a child's vulnerability if and when they do disclose, limit access to supports and services, and even restrict the child's ability to leave situations that are dangerous to them in the ways an adult can. In *The Write to Justice*, Fox describes several scenarios when the maltreatment she experienced was disclosed to others (2014). In Chapter 3 the sexual assault by a construction worker seemed to elicit no response at all when reported to a parent immediately after it happened (p. 29). In early adolescence the repeated assaults by groups of boys was reported to parents and school authorities but there was no real response commensurate with the crime of sexual assault (p. 33). As many as 65% of victims of child maltreatment and domestic violence report that abusers have used threats to harm the victim as well as the threat to harm siblings and family pets (MacIntosh, 2004). The threat of harm creates an atmosphere of fear and intimidation that makes disclosure to others far less likely to occur. The belief that harm may occur is powerful, whether or not action is ever taken. The kind of terror a child experiences when there is fear of harm of a sibling is described in *The Write to Justice* (Fox, 2014, p. 113, 218). When the victim hides to avoid the abuser it is often with feelings of terror and belief that a younger brother will be harmed.

It is important to acknowledge the way society defines crime, including crimes that are committed on or against children. The maltreatment of very young children is at times viewed as non-criminal primarily when it happens within the home or by family members. This view is, largely due to established social norms. Some of these norms are the result of:

- Minimization of the perception of damage (for instance if siblings are physically violent).
- The belief that children are resilient and will 'bounce back' from maltreatment.
- The belief that child abuse (unless it is grave and severe) and maltreatment like neglect is better handled by social agencies and in a non-criminal manner.
- Societal norms that go toward protecting the family create reluctance to involve the justice system even when that would be inevitable when police become involved in an adult matter perceived as criminal (Finkelhor, 2008).

According to the work of Seymour Levine as cited in Perry and Szalavits (2007), resilience in children is developmental and grows as the result of stress and nurturing experienced early in life. Memory is a critical component in the stress response. Once the brain has become sensitized to stress, it will tend to respond in a similar fashion even after minor exposure to stress, particularly if the stress is patterned and repetitive. Over the course of a lifetime, moderate, predictable and strengthening activation of stress systems actually contributes to human resilience. However, Perry explains that despite the commonly held perception that children are resilient, when it comes to recovering from early trauma, the opposite is true (2007).

Understanding Trauma

My analysis provides a context for understanding trauma experienced in early childhood and the distinctions between pain and meaning-mediated trauma (Finkelhor, 2008). First, I will discuss betrayal trauma theory and recent research into recovery from high betrayal trauma (HBT) when the perpetrator of the maltreatment is a trusted caregiver (Martin, 2013). In one important study by researchers from four American universities, trauma participants identified the cumulative type(s) of maltreatment they experienced (not the number of incidents). They identified the nature of the victim's relationship with the offender based on the distinctions defined as low-betrayal trauma (LBT), moderate-betrayal trauma (MBT), and high-betrayal trauma (HBT). The study also examined how trauma-related appraisals (how the victim understands or appraises the trauma), gender, and trauma symptomatology related

18

to these distinctions of betrayal trauma. While it is clear that victims of HBT are likely to suffer with significant symptomology associated with post-traumatic stress disorder (PTSD) including depression and dissociative memory disturbances, what is most significant to victim outcome is how the experiences are appraised (Martin, 2013).

> … when trauma appraisals were considered, appraisals were stronger predictors of outcomes than the cumulative trauma indices, suggesting that the manner in which trauma survivors think about and evaluate their experiences is an important component in determining prolonged distress, regardless of the trauma experienced (Martin, 2013 , p. 117).

As researchers gain insight into the potential for harm with children who are maltreated it is important to distinguish between *pain-mediated* and *meaning-mediated* traumas, particularly in children under the age of 3 years of age. According to the reconstructed memories of childhood trauma described in *The Write to Justice* (Fox, 2014) these began prior to the age of three, physical pain was a primary factor in determining how the trauma was experienced. Finkelhor suggests that even at such an early age where physical pain is the primary concern, the way a child will appraise or understand a traumatic event is likely to depend to some degree on how familiar the child is with the class of events as well as whether the exposure to trauma is an on-going risk (Finkelhor, 2008).

Although the (alleged) assaults happened on multiple occasions across the span of several years, these events were *pain-mediated* victimizations.

> REGRESSION – DAY FOUR
>
> I don't know if I can stand another day. I feel black and blue on the inside. Today I need comfort, but once again I breathe into my feelings.
>
> *I am hiding under a pile of dirty laundry. My Mommy has her monster eyes today. I want my Daddy but he has already left for work. I want to talk to my Papa on the phone. I'll be good, I won't say anything wrong. She finds me in the laundry and tells me I am a dirty girl. She takes me to the bedroom and puts my father's socks on my feet. She puts his tie around my neck. She has the scissors in her hands. She is going to fix me. I can't understand what she says any more. I close my eyes as the pain overwhelms me. I can only hear my own screaming now* (Fox, 2014, p. 100-101).

The repetition of certain rituals of abuse and the ability to anticipate 'what was coming' in a state of hyper vigilance suggests that there is also an element of *meaning-mediated* victimization. One important facet of the meaning-making process is the internalization of the belief that the events occurred when the child *self* was "a bad girl" (Fox, 2014, p. 100). The victimization described here typifies the criteria for *pain-mediated* victimization that can occur whenever any strong physical sensation occurs. Obviously, the painful experience of having scissors inserted vaginally and the other physical incidents graphically alluded to are typical of *pain-mediated* victimization (p. 100, 101). The symptoms of acute stress response evident after the traumatic incidents include overall anxiety, poor sleep patterns, chronic dissociation during waking hours (daydreaming), pronounced anxiety at the sound of another child crying in proximity and memory disruption typical of dissociation. Later, cathartic re-enactments of the trauma involved repetition of the words "I won't be bad" (p. 100, 101). These kinds of symptoms provide considerable insight into a child's developmental perspective. At the age of three the cognitive development of a child will permit only simple appraisals (the ability to give meaning to the experience of maltreatment and trauma) of events.

According to Janov, difficult childhood experiences are imprinted biologically as well as psychologically (Janov A. , 2006). Over the span of several decades Janov has written extensively in his effort to give evidentiary credibility to his *primal gating (line of consciousness) theory* of the way the unconscious mind carries memory imprints of trauma. Janov argues his findings are supported in neuroscience and his first research efforts were based on collaborative work with neuroscientist E. Michael Holden. The two men published their findings in *Primal Man: The New Consciousness* (Janov & Holden, 1975). In it, Holden insists that all psychosomatic illness is caused by unresolved, repressed memories and claims to have established that these memories exist on a cellular level and may reappear physically when the original trauma is re-experienced. Janov further describes brain function as intrinsically bound to memory storage, emotional adaptation to unresolved needs and trauma, and the subsequent psychosomatic expression of the resulting illness when feelings are repressed, dissociated from, and subverted. What is significant to Janov's contribution is his contention that verbalization, the use of language and words, will never provide a meaningful path toward the access and resolution of early trauma and unresolved need and pain (Janov A. , Primal Healing, 2006). He posits that the structure of the brain supports different types of consciousness and memory systems. The brainstem is the first part of the brain to develop and is responsible for basic survival impulses. In addition to controlling autonomic body functions like breathing and heartbeat, the brainstem responds to sensory information (Johns Hopkins Medicine, 2013). Janov insists that with the brainstem fully functional by the seventh month of gestation, pain such as birth trauma will be recorded and imprinted in the brainstem (Janov A. , Primal Healing, 2007). He calls this *first line* of consciousness pain and further suggests that many psychosomatic symptoms such as high blood pressure are an expression of that early influence on the brainstem.

Janov attributes the *second line* of consciousness to the limbic system as follows:

> The limbic system possesses some key structures that affect
> brain function, including the hippocampus, which is the
> guardian of emotional memory; the amygdala, which I
> believe may provide the "feeling" (sensation) of feeling, the

22

visceral components of feeling; and the hypothalamus and thalamus (Janov A. , Primal Healing, 2006, p. 66).

The limbic system is not linked to language, or to understanding what is being felt or sensed intellectually. Cognitive or intellectual development within the neocortex is still actively developing throughout the first three years of life. This *third line* of consciousness is the last to develop. Consequently, according to Janov, when early trauma occurs it imprints on a part of the brain inaccessible through talk therapies. In fact, he suggests that talk therapy may accomplish little more than a very temporary sense of relief and that even if the patient feels better, psychosomatic symptoms and illness may persist (Janov A. , Primal Healing, 2007). Janov's theory is that in order to achieve meaningful and lasting resolution of early trauma, it must be fully experienced in the context of the initial trauma, which will be on a feeling rather than a cognitive/verbal level (2007). Janov believes this is accomplished by catharsis or reliving the trauma.

Janov's early theories of memory storage of traumatic events are substantiated by current research in neurobiology today. One example of such research is a study led by a team at the University of California into memory storage and trauma (University of California - Irvine, 2005). Christa McIntyre and research professor James L. McGaugh, (who is referenced in Janov's *Primal Mind*) with the Center for the Neurobiology of Learning and Memory, have determined that only deeply arousing emotional experiences such as trauma are likely to be imprinted in the brain as a long term memory. Further, they were able to track a cascade of neurobiological activity that seems to essentially secure those memories in the brain's memory systems.

The cathartic experiences described in *The Write to Justice* (Fox, 2014, pp. 100, 101) seem to suggest agreement with Janov's theories in important ways. The long-term memories recovered and reconstructed are often visceral and non-verbal. The imprint on memory of physical pain and trauma was re-lived in the original context of experience in which it first occurred. The later attempts to understand the experiences and to attribute meaning to them through narrative, through language, were subsequent to the visceral experience of cathartic memory (Fox, 2014, p. Chapter 8).

Psychologist and leading narrative therapist Michael White emphatically rejects a theory of catharsis as a valid therapeutic tool for healing and recovery from childhood (and other forms) of trauma (White, 1994). He cautions that there is extreme risk to victims who are guided into revisiting original trauma as a therapeutic imperative, warning there is a real possibility for re-traumatization. One example of this as recounted in *The Write to Justice* is the decision made by psychotherapists to essentially abandon their client when catharsis reached a psychologically dangerous point, beyond their level of expertise.

While nothing in my life seemed to make any sense without those memories and everything fell into its own 'sense' with them, I couldn't just accept what was happening. I deteriorated more each day as my sense of self became increasingly fragile. Benet and Asu came to the difficult realization that it was irresponsible to continue with my therapy and I needed more than they were able to give. I was cut loose in a sea of my own overwhelming emotion as they abruptly discontinued my care (Fox, 2014, p. 101).

According to White, catharsis can reaffirm the dominant meanings or appraisal a victim has already taken from the original trauma and reinforce them. White suggests the critical element of meaning-making is excluded from the cathartic process. Moreover, White maintains there is a cultural aspect to asking people to go back to the original site of trauma and 'face it' that dishonours the strategies that they used successfully to survive at the time such as having the ability to "create self-sustenance" and "spirit themselves away in the mind" (p. 85). White asserts that there is no "expression of any experience that occurs outside a system of meaning" (p. 87). White does not acknowledge the integrative cognitive processes whereby the adult, after having experienced therapeutic catharsis, is able to make sense of their experiences and engage in appraisal, or re-appraisal of the meanings they attribute to events.

Mothers as Offenders in Child Maltreatment

Despite the perception that offenders in child maltreatment are predominantly male, a report by the Office on Child Abuse and Neglect and the U.S. Children's Bureau reveals a remarkably different picture indicating women are the primary offenders in cases of child abuse (Rosenberg, 2006). Fathers were involved in 36.8 percent of child maltreatment cases and mothers were involved in 64 percent of reported cases (Rosenberg, 2006). Another comprehensive report released in 2013, based on a review of 512,040 cases of reported child maltreatment submitted by 50 states, demonstrates that a statistical analysis of offender demographic based on gender shows that 53.5 percent of the offenders were female, 45.3 percent male and 1.1 percent unknown (Administration on Children, Youth and Families, 2013, p. 68). Overall, 80.3 percent of offenders were parents (2013, p. 72).

In the case of sexual abuse of children, the primary offender is male. However, in Canada, most of the females who offended were family members who abused their victims within their role as caretakers, and 25% were baby-sitters, teachers or day care workers. The majority of reported offenders were the biological mother. A statement released by the Calgary Communities Against Sexual Abuse (CASA) emphasizes "there is no difference in the severity of abuse by female sex offenders as compared to male sex offenders (Rudin et al., 1995)" (2014).

26

3. Feminist and Postmodernist Perspectives on Gendered Violence

One of the basic tenets of feminist analysis is the foundational understanding of how gendered power structures are intrinsic to the kinds of victimization most women experience in their personal lives, socially, culturally and economically. It is a fact that the vast majority of reported incidents of domestic abuse and sexual abuse are based on occurrences where the victims are female and the perpetrators are male. The prevalence of male offenders has lent itself to some feminist analysis that concluded that violence is a male gendered behaviour, used to create and maintain positions of power and authority. It is not my intention to dispute these legitimate and critical perspectives on oppression and power or to challenge the findings of feminisms informed by a postmodern perspective that recognizes that a hegemonic approach to gender analysis is likely to be more restrictive than informative. My contention is that we must be prepared to recognize that the same influences that contribute to oppressive and violent actions in men are likely to also affect women. Fitzroy suggests women will find ways of asserting their influence and 'power over' in the arenas they are able to do so (1999). For some women this will be in the home and their children will serve as their subordinates. Other women will assert their dominance through status and privilege in whatever social context they are able. We, men and women alike, will continue to do so as long as society at large endorses a valuing and devaluing of peoples based on power and subordination, gender and ability, race and religion and other divisive factors.

The perception of women as passive is problematic when women are viewed as weak and ineffectual. It is also problematic to the victims of violence and aggression perpetuated by women. When the perception of an individual offender and her victim is incongruent with the social or cultural ideal, reporting acts of aggression and harm can be very difficult.

There are many possibilities that account for how and why women are violent and abuse their children. The commonly cited Cycle of Violence theory first introduced in 1979 recognizes that many women (and men) who become abusers have experienced victimizations in their own childhood and are essentially acting out their experiences later with their victims (Walker, 2009). The Cycle of Violence theory is problematic however, because the vast majority of people who are victimized DO NOT go on to become abusers. There must be several complicated processes in place that contribute to the agency of an adult who becomes abusive of others. The Cycle of Violence theory neglects to consider all of these factors and can burden victims with an unfair belief that they are likely to become abusers.

Fitzroy reminds us that there are many "myths" (2001, p. 27) that attempt to explain the causality of violence in women, ranging from childhood trauma to having an excess of male hormones, and drug and alcohol abuse. In the case of *The Write to Justice* (Fox, 2014) there is also a suggestion of possible postpartum mental disorder. These explanations must be carefully evaluated. According to Fitzroy:

> Feminism quite legitimately asked men to consider issues of agency, choice, hegemonic masculinity, power, control, responsibility and motives within the behaviour of men as a gendered population. It is reasonable for us to extend such questions to our musing upon women's use of violence. The difficulty, however, is that simple binary explanations for women's violence, simple classifications of instrumental or explosive violence, 'bad', 'sad' or 'mad' women, are not sufficient to assist us in making sense of women's lives, their choices and their use of violence (Fitzroy L. , 2001, p. 27).

Women, Violence and Aggression

Western civilization has a long history of defining women as weak, passive and pure nurturers. These qualities are seen as an innate, natural part of being female both biologically and culturally. Caesar Lombroso, an early criminologist, did several studies attempting to correlate physical attributions with criminal and violent behaviour in both men and women. In his book *The Female Offender* 1889, Lombroso stated:

The Woman, as distinguished from the man... stands at one extremity or the other...being either perfectly normal or excessively anomalous. Consequently, women are very rarely criminal when compared with men but when criminal, they are infinitely worse (as cited by Hirsch, 1981, p. 140).

According to Klein (Klein in Hirsch 1981, p. 142) Freud believed that a woman, by nature, is destined to fulfil her social role by being charming, sweet, beautiful, a good wife and mother and that any rebellious attempt to change that is unhealthy. Pearson suggests this view of women has resulted in a "long tradition in our culture of depicting aggressive or criminal women as sexually perverse" (Pearson, When she was bad, 1997, p. 131). This is, in part, due to the way we define violence and aggression in women and our gender based, social construct of these qualities. According to a hegemonic male gendered style of measure, we see violence as direct and physical, in the form of punches kicks, pushes and brawls. An early study in 1968 in the United States submitted to the National Commission on the Causes and Prevention of Violence and reported by Pearson (1997, p. 14) found 70% of the respondents believed it was important for boys to have several fist fights while growing up. Despite the perception that women do not aggress, a study by anthropologist Victoria Burbank found that in more than 80 contemporary societies around the world, women did engage publicly in direct physical aggression (Pearson, 1997, p. 13).

Kaj Bjorkqvist, a Finnish psychologist interested in indirect aggression in adolescent girls, asked girls what they did to express anger or compete with rivals (Pearson, 1997, p. 17). They said they used such things as gossip, passing nasty notes, and exclusion from groups as basic power plays. Of course today, much of this behaviour could be characterized as bullying. Using a definition of aggression as *behaviour generally intended to inflict psychological or physical harm on another individual,* Pearson claims we have negated a whole class of injuries, commonly used or inflicted by girls and women.

In the Canadian Justice system, women are often sheltered from having to assume full, or at least equal responsibility for their violent or aggressive actions. According to a report by Statistics Canada in 2005, while more women than men were committing violent crimes and acts of aggressions, proportionately fewer women than men were charged and convicted of those crimes and women are often given shorter sentences when they are convicted (Statistics Canada 2005). When generating research data to gain insight into violence and aggression by women it is critical to include consideration of significant social, cultural and economic factors as contributors to violence, particularly when most aggression is committed against family members, including children and spouses (Statistics Canada, 2005).

The internalized belief that women, especially mothers, do not harm their children was powerful, persistent and difficult to overcome during the process of reconciling this social construct

31

with the reconstructed memories of abuse described in *The Write for Justice* (Fox, 2014). The gender explicit expectations of behaviour for both mother and daughter are dichotomous on virtually all levels of experience. There was a complexity to the veil of silence that protected the acts of violence against a young girl who came to believe that it happened because she was a *bad girl* (Fox, 2014). There was a complexity to the appraisal that the *badness* was somehow explicitly tied to gender. While the nature of the abuse was sexualized (in assaults focused on the genitals), it was not sexual according to typical constructs of understanding. To the external world, the image of a passive, obedient and good mother and her good daughter was equally as powerful as was the internalized identity of being a 'bad girl'. The only way to survive as a child was to adapt to the dissociative and psychotic episodes where my mother became violent and aggressive, by learning to become equally able to disconnect from the pain experience. Here, dissociation was a patterned behaviour and a learned survival strategy or, as White would perhaps suggest, a spiriting away of the mind (White, 1994, p. 85). Writing the story in autoethnography is an important, indeed critical opportunity to integrate the pain-mediated experience of trauma through meaning-making appraisals and to engage in a healing process. In fact, the writing itself changes the story to one of resilience and recovery.

Postpartum Mental Disorder and Child Harm

A thorough review and discussion of the legal implications and provisions for defence in cases of child harm by mothers, primarily infanticide as sequelae to postpartum mental disturbance after childbirth, is beyond the scope of this paper. However, it is important to provide a legal context to the discussion presented here. In a comprehensive review of postpartum mental disorder and the law, Langer discusses the legal provisions for defence when a mother harms her child within the first year of childbirth or lactation. She argues "postpartum mental disorder is treated in law with an ambivalent mix of compassion, dismissiveness and outrage" (Langer, 2012, p. 358).

In Canada, there are legal provisions in the Criminal Code of Canada in Section 233 as follows:

> A female person commits infanticide when by a wilful act or omission she causes the death of her newly-born child, if at the time of the act or omission she is not fully recovered from the effects of giving birth to the child and by reason thereof or of the effect of lactation consequent on the birth of the child her mind is then disturbed. R.S., c. C-34, s. 216 (Criminal Code of Canada, 2014).

Langer discusses a number of problems in the current provisions found in Canadian law that illustrate a lack of consistency or universality in understanding the diminished capacity of a mentally ill woman to appreciate that her actions, while in a state of imbalance, are morally wrong (2012). There are problems with the interpretation of responsibility for those actions and with how the application of infanticide law has not been consistent in Canadian courtrooms. In the case of infanticide law, the harm is clear when it has resulted in the death of a child. However, these provisions in the law do not extend to cases of harm to a child that has not resulted in death, or when the harm extends beyond the one year provision in law as was the case with Margaret in *The Write to Justice* (Fox, 2014).

Langer suggests that postpartum mental disorders occur within the larger social context of idealized motherhood (2012). She reminds us that childbirth itself is a major life event, one that demands change and adjustment in intimate relationships, financial status and contributes to problems of social isolation. It is of particular significance to this writer that the social anxiety leading to fear and shame surrounding pregnancy is an important causal factor with infanticide:

A common variation is a young mother overcome with fear and shame about an undeclared pregnancy, and who commits neonaticide (Langer, 2012, p. 375).

The changes experienced during pregnancy and through childbirth are complex. They are indeed social in context. There is evidence in neuroendocrinology of changes to the brain itself that corresponds to specific hormonal changes as early as the first trimester of pregnancy. In fact, the levels of prolactin and oxytocin, hormones associated with the potential for human bonding between love partners and between mother and child, begin to change significantly in the first trimester (Feldman, 2012). There is some evidence that a stable oxytocin level in the first trimester is an important predictor of a successful and stable bonding period between a mother and her new infant (2012).

The presumption of postpartum mental disorder offers an explanation for the horrific, early maltreatment experienced by the researcher *self* at the hands of Margaret as remembered (primarily) during cathartic therapy sessions (Fox, 2014). At the very least, it is suggested that the pregnancy and childbirth are pivotal and destabilizing events. The first chapters in *The Write to Justice* (Fox, 2014) describe the social, cultural and economic reality faced by a young woman living in the city of Toronto in the 1950s when she meets her 'soon-to-be' husband. Living in a postwar era, women's lives were expected to evolve around plans to find a husband and have a family whereby they would find their ultimate fulfillment as the devoted homemaker. The media focused a message of domestic bliss to a targeted audience through women's magazines that seemed to offer sage advice on how to *be* the ideal woman. Women could read expert advice and learn about what would make *normal* (idealized) women happy, about fashion and beauty, tips on how to perform domestic tasks so that their homes were filled with the smell of home cooked meals, surfaces sparkled and happiness was a new kitchen appliance. The 1950s were a time of transition around how to raise children, with mixed messages that on one hand required absolute devotion and attention to every need a child may have, and on the other hand to setting up a schedule that allowed a woman to tend to her child while maintaining a home and responding to the needs of her husband. Always, she was to put on her best appearance in hopes it would convince everyone, including herself, that her world was a happy place. Margaret read her magazines religiously before she was married and for years after and embodied the ideals of womanhood to the best of her ability. Her failure to realize the ideal was not hers alone.

It was the era that followed the publication by Helene Deutsch, titled *The Psychology of Women - A Psychoanalytical Interpretation* in 1944. Deutsch wrote that femininity could be achieved when women abandoned their personal dreams and ambitions and sought personal fulfillment through supporting the activities and ambitions of their husbands and sons (as cited by Held, 2012). Deutsch defined the good mother as a woman who had the capability to tolerate suffering. Certainly, this seemed to be a model of womanhood embraced by Margaret (Fox, 2014) when she married in January of 1956 and gave birth to her daughter in July of that year. This was, nevertheless, a period of her life shrouded by secrets and shame that arrived in the form of an infant girl, born only 7 months after the day of the wedding and weighing in at a healthy birth weight of 8 pounds and clearly not premature. Chapter One of *The Write to Justice* (Fox, 2014) describes Margaret as the daughter of an old country, Scottish Presbyterian couple with strong cultural and religious convictions. To conceive a child outside of the sanctity of marriage was a sin in the eyes of her family and to Margaret as well. The thought of anyone knowing the child was conceived illegitimately was unbearable and Margaret attempted to persuade family and friends that her daughter was born two months premature weighing slightly more than 4 pounds. To make matters worse, the new family moved into her parent's home only two weeks after she gave birth. Ronald, the new husband and father, would go back to school to pursue his goals and ambitions and work toward becoming a school teacher. Margaret would stay home alone during the days with her mother and the object of her shame, her infant daughter (2014).

Despite the best of intentions to achieve a measure of good motherhood she expected of herself, Margaret was living in a precarious situation. She had abandoned any goals and dreams of her own. She undoubtedly felt isolated and abandoned as her new husband left for teacher's college every day in the interest of becoming a professional. She believed Ronald was inherently more capable than she was to have such dreams and that he was intellectually her superior. She felt fortunate to be married to such a man. There was little room to complain about her situation. She would 'grin and bear it' as her daily affirmation. Who could share her private, tormented thoughts if she was to maintain the image of a dutiful wife and mother?

For all of the advice she gleaned from women's magazines; there was virtually no mention of postpartum depression or postpartum psychosis in the media until 1952. According to their comprehensive review of print media over a period of 50 years, Held and Rutherford (2012) determined that during the 1950s, postpartum depression was essentially characterized as the *third-day blues:*

> The Ladies' Home Journal (Bundesen, 1952) warned mothers that their next psychological hurdle, after overcoming the third-day blues, was to adjust to a household routine that was dominated by the baby's demands. However, the author noted, mothers were often upset to find that they rarely had time they could call their own. The remedy was an understanding husband who would take over some of the baby care responsibilities in the evening or on weekends so that mom would get a few hours to read, rest, or visit with friends. This, the article noted, "is all that is needed, usually, to restore her buoyant spirits" (p. 87) (Held, 2012, p. 110).

It is evident there were several risk factors that would have the potential to affect Margaret. There was a lack of meaningful social support despite being married and having a family of her own. The reality of financial dependency on her parents, while Ronald was in teacher's college, would be challenging for any family. Margaret had no privacy and no way of concealing this large baby who could hardly be represented as premature when she weighed twice the birth weight Margaret entered into her personal baby birth record. Every sound the baby made seemed to announce to the world she was there. This situation brought a sense of public shame, with a child who could not be hidden and no amount of 'grin and bear it' would make the situation comfortable.

I reflected on my mother's life and recognized many of the risk factors that would have the potential to affect her. Certainly there was a lack of significant social support. My mother lived with her own parents in their home. She was married, had a new husband and child but was still dependent on her parents financially. There would have been little opportunity for privacy as a married couple. My mother was living with the object of her own deep feelings of shame – namely an infant daughter who could not be hidden and was there for the whole world to see, all eight pounds of me. My father was in school pursuing a whole new career. How did his absence day to day affect my mother? How did all of this stress affect her hormonal levels? Was there ever a diagnosis of postpartum psychosis? I am certain there was not. Little was known about the condition in 1956. I find it unlikely she would have shared the thoughts and feelings she may or may not have recognized as abnormal.

The woman the world saw as a capable, competent and good mother was not the woman I was with when doors and windows were closed, drapes were drawn and nobody else was home. That woman muttered and rambled nonsensically at times. That woman had eyes that could look frantic. That woman was often in a state where everything she did to me held a highly symbolic context and her efforts to 'clean me' were almost ritualistic.

That woman was lost, desperate and alone.

But so was her daughter. (Fox, The Write to Justice, 2014, pp. 128-129)

In the midst of the social negation of women and their needs as individuals, the message persisted in the media that postpartum depression, the baby blues or the third-day blues, were quite simply the result of a woman's failure to adjust to motherhood and the demands of an infant. Huge numbers of women in the 1950s reported severe and traumatic experiences in hospitals through the management of childbirth, ranging from indifference by medical staff to the horrors of being strapped to a bed while flat on their backs and other ultimately dehumanizing experiences (Held, 2012). The difficult period so many women report once they return to their homes and to the demands of a new baby, husband and other family members was attributed to character flaws in any woman who couldn't keep in step with the changes and expectations placed on them. To admit one was struggling was tantamount to admitting to failure as a woman.

The explanation of postpartum psychosis as a motive or reason for a woman to harm her infant is more than simply a biochemical response to pregnancy and childbirth. It is perhaps best described in *Time* magazine and attributed to sociologist Ann Oakley:

> The recipe for depression, she says, is to create an unrealistic myth about motherhood, offer unfeeling medical care, and then set the new mother down in a social system that offers her little support for her new child and new role. Oakley, the mother of three, thinks childbirth is so oversold as women's greatest achievement that women believe something is wrong with them if they have ambivalent feelings after giving birth. (Postbirth Blues, 1980, p. 58) (as cited by Held, 2012)

Compounded by the circumstances surrounding the birth of her daughter, it is little wonder that Margaret experienced profound isolation and despair that led to the victimization of both mother and daughter - both were victims without a voice.

Difficult Knowledge

Feminism has contributed to an understanding of how women's knowing and knowledge are embedded in their lived experiences and that existing power structures and dynamics can either encourage, or discourage the ways a story is told and heard because the connection between knowledge and power relations silences so many girls and women who are not in a position to reap the benefits of relative privilege that can be associated with being identified with dominant social groups (middle class, able-bodied, white, etc.). The academic study of feminist epistemology (ways of knowing) has resulted in a body of information that suggests women's gender specific experiences are not well acknowledged or understood Elizabeth Anderson suggests the following factors are significant to feminist epistemology:

Various practitioners of feminist epistemology and philosophy of science argue that dominant knowledge practices disadvantage women by (1) excluding them from inquiry, (2) denying them epistemic authority, (3) denigrating their "feminine" cognitive styles and modes of knowledge, (4) producing theories of women that represent them as inferior, deviant, or significant only in the ways they serve male interests, (5) producing theories of social phenomena that

42

render women's activities and interests, or gendered power relations, invisible, and (6) producing knowledge (science and technology) that is not useful for people in subordinate positions, or that reinforces gender and other social hierarchies (Anderson E. , 2012).

Women who are disadvantaged, including aboriginal women, lesbians, religious minority women, poor women, disabled women and all women who are marginalized are therefore less likely to be visible and their stories are less likely to be heard. The stories of women and girls victimized through violence, including the violence of other women, are silenced and therefore become 'difficult knowledge' when expressed and described. Consequently, understanding a woman's story requires considered attention and sensitivity on the part of the audience, with a willingness to more fully comprehend the meaning of lived experience. The complexity of the story asks the reader to be willing to deconstruct inherent knowledge and biases in order to more fully appraise the writer's story. In doing so we encounter the taboo of difficult knowledge that silences women who have lived experiences that are inconsistent with gender and cultural hegemony. Likewise, when a researcher engages in the narrative process, it is important to deconstruct her own biases and limitations through a reflective process to better gain insight and acquire meaning. The reflective process demands a careful mapping and creation of an inventory of social, political and cultural dominant discourses that create a terrain of context that determines how we understand ourselves and others.

There are important representations of difficult knowledge explored in *The Write to Justice* (Fox, 2014). Previously in this chapter I have discussed some of the myths and misconceptions that inform our social response to violence in women. Feminism has been at times reluctant to engage in open discursive investigation of violence in women, upholding traditional, modernist views of gender that suggest women are first victims of violence and that agency in women who are violent is reactive (Fitzroy L. , 2001) (Shaw & Dubois, 1995). Certainly, the predominance of female victimization upholds the feminist and postmodern analysis of a power dynamic that creates disadvantage and all of the difficulties associated with that. The personal lived experience of abortion is another example of difficult knowledge that has proven to be highly divisive among all of society. Feminists have often resisted acknowledgment of analysis that does not uphold a pro-choice position that includes abortion on demand. This can have a profound influence on women and their telling of stories that describe difficult experiences with abortion.

Reproductive medicine and technology are issues discussed at critical points throughout the life story expressed in *The Write to Justice* (Fox, 2014). There is thick description of the lived experience of abortion, sexuality as an exchange for survival, chemical

44

sterilization through high doses of the drug Depo Provera, motherhood, reproductive technology and finally surrogacy. There is a fairly robust description of some of the contextual stressors that contribute many of the challenges and circumstances experienced across a lifetime. At the age of fourteen there was no legal or moral obligation to include a minor in the decision making process that was incumbent on the parents and medical personnel who were involved in giving consent for an abortion.

In a concerted effort to avoid the pitfalls of 'victim feminism', the discourse of choice shifts the focus away from patriarchal structures of oppression to one of individual bids for freedom (Murphy, 2012). Murphy suggests that choice feminism as an empowerment discourse posits that "every individual is free to choose and that choice is empowering, no matter what the choice actually is (p. 21)." There is an assumption that individuals can and will have access to the resources that empower personal agency and autonomy. This is naïve and insensitive to the real obstacles facing many women in North America and around the world and the subjugation women still contend with in many cultures. As poststructural feminists argue, human actions and agency are contingent on embedded, existing social practices, discourses, and institutions - the dynamics of power relations (see the work of Judith Butler). Choice is only empowering if and when you have the ability to act on your decisions and that may be more reflective of relative privilege for a select few than of universally valuable principles. There is a further assumption that given the 'right' to choose, many women will opt for abortion for a host of reasons. In fact, when a woman becomes pregnant in less than optimal circumstances there is an implied expectation that she will, at the very least, be offered abortion as an option.

The reflective process of evocative autoethnography in *The Write to Justice* allows the writer to express, through a discourse of feelings, the direct experience of childhood maltreatment and the subsequent harm suffered as sequelae in multiple victimizations including abortion, homelessness, rape and chemical sterilization in an institutional setting (Fox, 2014). Prior to writing autoethnography, the limited opportunity to give voice and expression to the experiences of harm that began in early childhood was followed by an ever-increasing loss of voice throughout adolescence and early adulthood. In some ways, beginning the process of writing my story felt as though I was writing from the proverbial grave where my family was concerned. Narrative inquiry through autoethnography provides a critical opportunity to re-situate knowledge and meaning-making through a migration of identity from that of the *bad girl without a voice and legal right of personhood* to assuming of an identity that honours the resources and strengths of a *woman with a voice* who has insights and knowledge that are important to share.

4. Evocative Autoethnography

Feminism and the field of psychology have made significant contributions to an awareness of power dynamics and the subjectivity and potential for bias on the part of the researcher (Etherington, 2004, p. 21). Feminist discourse analysis has deepened our understanding of how dominant knowledge practices affect those who are disadvantaged or whose personal experience is not in line with cultural hegemony and results in their exclusion from inquiry and the denial of their epistemic and discursive authority. Moreover, the use of special language and terminology that maintains a division between common language and embodied experience can result in expropriation of authentic voice: they do more to maintain power structures than to empower individuals (Frank, 2013, p. np). Despite critical concerns over the subjective writing and potential for researcher bias in autoethnography, there are times when the specialized language of academic research conducted according to a more conventional model of objectivity, fails to deepen our understanding and insight. The voices of victims who describe and disclose their personal stories can directly inform our sensitivity to the way embodied experiences of trauma and injury are lived and understood.

Social constructivism has contributed to the understanding that our beliefs are constructs of meaning (Etherington, 2004, pp. 22-23) and are influenced by such factors as race, gender, economic status, class, education and culture (Ellis, 2011, p. 3). Davetian suggests

47

that people are also influenced by their own "personal biographies and unresolved emotions" as much as by cultural factors such as race, status, and religion (2009, p. 93). With an understanding of these influences on our own personal beliefs and the beliefs of others, as researchers we can begin to reflect on our subjective experiences and biases in order to gain insight into their meanings (Etherington, 2004, p. 23). The social researcher who chooses autoethnography as a method of qualitative research faces a number of challenges. Several theorists have stated their objections to autoethnography as a valid form of social research, offering comprehensive critiques and rationales from polarized perspectives. Leon Anderson opines that researcher bias within the subjective experience is problematic and can lead to what he calls narcissistic writing when the author is "self-absorbed" (Analytic Autoethnography, 2006, p. 385). Nevertheless, postmodern and poststructural influences on contemporary social research have created an interdisciplinary interest in the lived, emotional experience (Anderson, 2006, p. 373). Autoethnography has evolved as a methodology that places narrative writing of the self within a social context (Etherington, 2004, p. 140). As researchers became interested in sensitizing others to social, cultural and political realities that could not easily be expressed through more sterile and impersonal methodologies, distinct disciplinary lines began to merge. Ellis et al. describe how interest grew when researchers realized personal experience and the stories told are "complex, constitutive, meaningful phenomena that taught morals and ethics,

48

introduced unique ways of feeling, and helped people make sense of themselves and others" (Ellis C. A., 2011, p. 2).

The Phenomenology of Experience and Meaning-making

Hermeneutical phenomenology places the lived experience at the starting point of investigation into the subjective process of forming unique meanings and understandings of events (Griffin & May, 2012). It can be said that the phenomenologist, like the autoethnographer, is interested in the subjectivity of experience (Englander, 2012). For the purpose of this discussion I will accept the definition of hermeneutical phenomenology found in the Stanford Encyclopedia of Philosophy provided by Hanson (2013)

> Hermeneutical phenomenology is a method of philosophical inquiry aimed at clarifying how background ideas, practices, and beliefs shape our interpretations of the world (including our activities in the world). Martin Heidegger called his method in Being and Time (1962) hermeneutical phenomenology in order to emphasize that the proper role of philosophical inquiry is to make explicit the implicit practices that constrain our understanding of what exists. Traditional hermeneutics is the art of interpreting texts by putting them in context, i.e., if one wants to understand a 18th century British novel, it helps to understand the ideas, institutional arrangements, and

historical events contemporary to the novel (Palmer 1969). Phenomenology is the attempt to study experience (whether objectively or subjectively) free from entrenched theoretical models that selectively attend to certain features of our experience while ignoring others. Hence, hermeneutical phenomenology aims to make explicit the "inescapable frameworks" through which we interpret our experience (Taylor 1989) (Hansen, 2013, p. sec. 2.1.1).

Hermeneutical phenomenologists are interested in understanding how the perception of reality is constructed and ways the world and lived experience are interpreted within the context of time, place, culture, emotion and other relevant factors. Patton, as cited by Seidman, states that "Without context there is little possibility of exploring the meaning of an experience (Patton, 1989)" (Seidman, 1998, p. 17). Leon Anderson's critique of evocative autoethnography suggests there can be a problem with losing sight of larger social worlds when the focus of study is on the researcher *self* who fails to adequately represent others (2006, p. 385). According to Anderson, "the preeminent goal of evocative autoethnography" is to "take us to the depths of personal feeling, leading us to be emotionally moved and sympathetically understanding" (Anderson, 2006, p. 385). He argues that the problem of maintaining a focus on the self as subject is that it fails to provide an analytic social context permitting the social researcher

50

to develop nomothetic or "generalized theoretical understandings" of social processes (p. 385). The focal point of Anderson's argument is that his own concept of 'analytic ethnography' is an approach that prevents the researcher/author from digressing into self-absorption (p. 385). He claims that analytic autoethnography is grounded in self-experience, but reaches beyond the subjective experience of self to include the larger social world. In so doing, he suggests his approach prevents the problem of narcissism in writing through inclusion of dialectic exchanges with others, whereby there is a researcher commitment to an analytic agenda (p. 386).

What Anderson fails to fully consider is that phenomenological research is intended to provide information that *can* be broadly applied to a population that has experienced the phenomenon of interest such as the embodied or lived experience of childhood victimization. A person who has experienced the phenomenon of interest, even when that person is the researcher *self*, is representative of that population (in the absence of evidence that would suggest they are not). It is the lived experience of a phenomenon that is of interest to the researcher (Englander, 2012), but analysis of that phenomenon can be applied to developing nomothetic or "generalized theoretical understandings" of social processes (Anderson, 2006, p. 385).

Narrative Expression

Human language expresses the cultural influences individuals are exposed to – especially during the important formative years. The study of biology and advances in neuroscience firmly establish the ways in which humans have the ability to acquire language, but it is human *culture* that is taught and learned through language (Budani, 2007). Language serves several fundamental and day to day purposes. It is instrumental and regulatory as we learn to identify the things we want, learn how to ask for them and communicate our needs and desires to others. We learn to use language in an interactional way as we develop social relationships. Personal opinions and feelings are expressed and explored through language. This developmental process can also be directed toward imaginative and creative idea making through play, fantasy creation, dramatization and more. Information gathering and sharing through language can lead to heuristic development and enable a sense of independence in truth or fact gathering (2007). Language defines and expresses self and culture as well as the individual and society.

According to Davis (2004), narrative storytelling does more than simply communicate the facts and chronology of an event. The telling of the story, or authoring of the narrative, allows us the opportunity to actively participate in cultural expression and thus becomes "the means by which we interpret and answer the world" (par. 6, 2004). Davis suggests that the act of storytelling involves first selecting which story will be authored or shared. The way the story is told involves a process of interpretation and reflection which itself creates a new experience beyond being a repetitious, factual recounting of something that has occurred in the past.

This process of telling is a reframing of personal experience that is the premise of narrative therapy as first theorized by therapist Michael White in 1995 (Goldenberg & Goldenberg, 2013). According to Goldenberg and Goldenberg, re-authoring a story allows the individual to explore new ways of understanding the story they tell, and the choices they make in terms of what meaning they attribute to the events. Family narratives and assumptions ultimately result in a kind of collective worldview that suggests certain people and situations are positive or negative. Narrative storytelling can provide an opportunity to externalize those beliefs by creating an object that is suitable for contemplation. When life experiences are reviewed they can be evaluated and contribute to new understanding. That new understanding will change the way the story itself is written and the way the life experience is integrated into future choices and actions (Goldenberg & Goldenberg, 2013).

Narrative expression can help the writer to externalize conversations within *self* that develop and form through relationship and interaction with others. Individual identities as *self* are not single voiced. In fact, the many voices of relational others actively contribute to personal, internal discourse. We are *who* we are in relationship with others. This is a highly changeable construct and not simply a static state of being. When individuals internalize the voices of others into an identity as a *self*, it can be challenging, yet extremely useful to recognize the source of the voice within and from there make choices about the authority and placement of that voice in our present lives and dreams for the future (Russell, 2002).

Psychologist and leading narrative therapist Michael White embraces the concept of re-membering originally introduced by anthropologist Barbara Myerhoff (Russell, 2002). In her work with members of the elderly Jewish community in California, Myerhoff used the term re-membering to describe a type of recollection that brings together a sense of significant individuals who belong in one's life story. Michael White introduced the term re-membering into narrative therapy and suggested that people's identities are shaped by what he referred to metaphorically as a 'club of life' (as cited by Russell, 2002). We give certain individuals a hierarchy of status in our lives, regardless of whether that influence has been harmful or supportive. Narrative expression can be a way to externalize those internal conversations whereby we hear and interact with the voices of and interactions with others. Through narrative inquiry we are able to make conscious decisions about the status and influence we choose to give them in our present understanding. This contributes to what White describes as a migration of identity that can be critical to victims of childhood maltreatment who still suffer from the powerful influence of people who contributed to a negative understanding of self and personal terrain (Russell, 2002).

The Interactive Process

Autoethnography is not simply the documentation of a chronological account of events, occurrences and experiences that have occurred in a linear sequence in the past. While historical accounts suggest a context of time and place within the writing process, reflective writing and expression is the process of structuring and re-structuring the meaning of lived experience. Autoethnography is both the product and the process. According to Maynes, Pierce & Laslett (2012), the interdisciplinary analysis of narrative stories has brought otherwise marginalized voices forward into our awareness. We, the audience, have the opportunity to watch, listen to and contemplate on the meaning of the experiences the storyteller shares. While this gives us a greater awareness of the social and personal influences that contributed to the development and interpretation of the storyteller's life event, that awareness and contemplation informs our own understandings and shapes the meanings we attribute to those circumstances. The story as a factual chronology of events offers only one aspect of narrative value. The meanings that are attributed to the events by both the storyteller and the audience are of even greater significance.

In the law, legal storytelling is often removed from victims and offenders alike as the story is honed to present a credible version of truth (Sherwin, 1994). The narrative is re-written by authoritative experts (usually lawyers and their legal assistants) and the story may no longer reflect what is meaningful to the person whose life experience is going on public record. Likewise, in therapeutic relationships, there is a risk that the therapist may assume a position of primacy and become directive in the meaning-making process of creating narrative. This may inhibit, and even render meaningless the process of story making if the insights generated are not authentic. In academic writing there is a risk that the institution or other scholars and disciplinary traditions can represent the authoritative voice that is directive in the language a writer/researcher uses, the content of the story told and the meaning-making process. It can be beneficial to draw on process guidelines borrowed from Elizabeth Anderson's recommendations for collaborative research and narrative inquiry (Anderson E. , 2012). The first suggestion is that the parties involved in storytelling (creation of narrative) recognize that they are engaged in a collaborative process with their audience that is bound to be reciprocal. Each will contribute to the awareness of the other. There should be conscious effort made to assure there is no power dynamic that maintains primacy of the reader, a therapist or any other voice of authority (Anderson E. , 2012).

Digital Storytelling and Contemporary Media

Thus far in this paper I have only briefly acknowledged the oral tradition of storytelling (Budani, 2009). As Davis states, "The
56

intonation, gestures, expressions, and accents of the storyteller convey the emotional significance of the story along with the words" (2004, par. 18). As feminist epistemology informs us, learning is situated differently depending on a host of factors including gender, age, interests, embodiment of experience, cognitive styles and worldview (Anderson E. , 2012). Epistemology informs the narrative process and it is important to recognize the role that the selection of medium can play to satisfy both the storyteller and the audience – each with their own situated knowledge.

The Center for Digital Storytelling, founded by Joe Lambert in 1998 with a group of artists in the San Francisco area, is devoted to empowering the telling of personal stories toward positive social change. The Center has developed into an international non-profit corporation that is "dedicated to surfacing authentic voices around the world through group process and participatory media creation, to share and bear witness to stories that lead to learning, action, and positive change" (Lambert, 2013).

Prior to public access to the internet and the development of personal computers and technology that supported relatively affordable video production in the 1990's, film making was an expensive enterprise dominated by interests that did little to deliver authentic first person narratives to the public domain (Davis, 2004). Now, with the universal availability of cell phones and personal devices that have cameras with video and recording capabilities, the genre of digital storytelling has assumed a place in social media and even has some specific guidelines for creation. The digital story normally begins with a storyboard that allows the storyteller to create frame by frame narrative and to select images and sound that help to tell the story. The ability to combine these elements of narrative can have strong appeal, given the delivery as a "screen media" (Davis, 2004, p. par. 19). Social media like Facebook® and websites such as YouTube® and Vimeo® provide avenues for distribution of screen media previously unavailable, and easily accessible to the general public.

One such YouTube® video, *Child Abuse Story* (Stop It With Me, 2013), provides an important example of a victim making use of digital media to give voice to trauma she experienced as a child. Narrative expression and disclosure of early trauma through digital storytelling can be a powerful tool for healing and recovery and to generate social awareness. Digital media includes elements of the written word, visual images and sound, and can engage youth and other interested members of the public through easy access to productions through popular social media. More research is necessary that explores the use of digital storytelling for expression of trauma that occurred at a developmental age where language alone may not serve to convey the full impact of the story and for those who face other challenges to using the written word. The narrative presented in the video *Child Abuse Story* (2013) states in visual print that *Today, She is Just About Piecing Together What*

Happened. We read, and in fact *see* how the trauma lingers even though the abuser is gone, through what is a multisensory experience for the audience. The images convey the trauma and the choice of music is a powerful enhancement to the victim's story. The story is told in the third person without naming the victim. At the beginning of the video, the identity of the victim is fictionalized as a *Princess Who Lost Her Fairytale Ending.*

The production of *The Write to Justice* (Fox, 2014) is a 2:24 minute digital video, published on YouTube® and was created as an enhancement to the narrative text of the book. The music that plays in the background was selected for the somewhat pensive or reflective mood it suggests. The choice of childhood images connects to the narrative and suggests there is more to 'the story'. Childhood trauma is often hidden behind the appearance of socially acceptable, day to day family life. In this video, the victim is named as the researcher *self* and the abuser is identified as my mother. One must exercise abundant caution and give due ethical consideration to the decision to make these productions public.

5. Creative Non-fiction

There are several justifications for writing autoethnography as fiction and creative non-fiction where salient aspects to the story, such as the names and identities of subjects, are changed. These changes are often made to protect the subject and relational others from potential harm. Nevertheless, one must reconcile the question of truthful disclosure and representation of fact with the idea of fiction and creative non-fiction. The novel *Bastard Out of Carolina* is a powerful example of creative non-fiction as author Dorothy Allison writes in the narrative voice of her character Ruth Anne "Bone" Boatwright, telling her story of childhood sexual abuse, illegitimacy and poverty (Allison, 1992). Allison's fictionalized account gives voice to painful memories and experiences without the limitations implied by the use of 'real' names and identities. She sacrifices the disclosure of identifying information in order to protect her ability to share the greater, more important truth of her lived experience and difficult knowledge. The reader is able to engage more fully with the story by hearing it through the voice of "Bone". Without having to assume the responsibility for judging if the story is told truthfully from a factual standpoint, the reader is free to engage emotionally with the experiences described.

Leigh Gilmore expresses concern that narrative in a memoir has limitations for authors who choose to write stories of trauma and testimony (2001). She describes a 'confession boom' that resulted in a large number of published memoirs at the turn of the millennium. Many of these memoirs told difficult stories of pain, suffering and oppression. In some cases, telling the truth of traumatic experience invited harsh social judgments. Instead of providing an outlet for expression, the author would experience secondary victimization and trauma. Fiction, however, provides an outlet for the important truth that compels narrative disclosure of trauma and painful life experience. When there are potential legal implications to establishing the credibility of a memoir written about trauma or oppression at the hands of another, the risks of publishing factually could outweigh the benefits. An author writing of traumatic injury for instance, may elect to change the facts of relative time and place and names of others involved in order to give way to the more important truth. Such was the case in my decision to change the name of Kenny in *The Write to Justice* (Fox, The Write to Justice, 2014).

In *The Write to Justice*, Chapter 7, (Fox, 2014) the story of Kenny is written as creative non-fiction. Kenny was a young Albanian Moslem man whose sister was murdered in Toronto by her father in an apparent 'honour-killing.' The gruesome details were made public during the trial that eventually led to their father being convicted of manslaughter. It was a laborious process to find archived newspaper articles that could verify certain details surrounding the killing. After months of searching for information, I finally located and made copies of news articles found in the Toronto Star newspaper archives (Toronto Star, accessed 2014).

Although the articles could establish the veracity of the story of a young girl murdered in what is often characterized as an honour killing after she refused to accept that she had been 'sold by her father' to marry someone she didn't love, I realized I could not use them in the book even with proper permissions from the Toronto Star. The threat of harm still exists for family members and I recently learned of at least 5 more murders within the extended family that had occurred over the past three decades. To publicly expose Kenny and his current wife and children to being named would serve no good purpose and place these people potentially in harm's way. While no other details are changed in the way the story is told, the names of these individuals are changed. This would not guarantee absolute anonymity and offers only superficial protection. If anyone were really motivated to identify Kenny and his family they could do so, albeit with great difficulty. I also changed the names and identifying information of others described in the book but the elements of the story that were germane to the process were written factually.

Perceptions of Truth

The concept of truth in narrative has been an important subject for legal meaning makers as well as for social science researchers. In the context of legal testimony, some details of a story will be disclosed while others are discarded if they do not serve the version of the truth presented. Sherwin claims there is an important moment where human actors make decisions about what the story is, and that *becomes* the story (1994). In autobiographical writing, as well as in criminal law, Bruner suggests it is the ability to determine what is credible and which truth is likely to be accepted that will determine what will be disclosed (1995). Sherwin argues that the problem of truth in law is not in the process of telling the story, or even with decisions about which details to include and which to leave out (1994). The modernist way of thinking is interested in categorizing dichotomous options for determining if a story is true or false and if a human actor is guilty or innocent. It is this way of thinking in "stark polarities" that satisfies our desire to interpret the truth of a situation in the simplest of terms (Sherwin, 1994, p. 42).

Bruner suggests both reader and listener alike ask if the *verisimilitude* of the story, in the context in which it is presented, rings true (1995). Simply stated, is the story believable? Even when a story is told factually it must reflect historical and cultural markers of accuracy to be accepted as a valid and relevant exploration. This is especially true in autoethnography. The truth of the situation is important, but it may be quite complex. The determination of truth will depend on the socially complex perspectives of those who hear or read autobiographical stories, the audience. Sherwin suggests it is important to consider that apparently conflicting stories may simultaneously be true (1994). He cautions that our own involvement in the process as the audience may work more toward "reality-making" (p. 42) than to simply be passive receivers of factual information. As we bring our own complex perspectives with us as a reader or audience, we become a directive participant in the story itself. The urge to simplify the sense of right and wrong and to assess truth and falsehood lies in our desire to avoid situations that destabilize our own beliefs and values. When we are protecting our own stories (developed out of our cultural, social and individual experiences), we are far less likely to consider versions of the truth that are difficult to reconcile ourselves to (Sherwin, 1994).

Does Changing the Story in Creative Non-fiction Mean we have Changed our Perception of Truth?

In autoethnography, narrative expression involves a process of writing the *self* retrospectively. According to Bruner the *self* of this moment, the *now self* is concerned with a retrospective view of possibilities and choices, experiences and meaning-making that is in actuality a *metaphor for the self* (1995). It is not the *actual self* that is written, it is a collective representation of actions, decisions, meanings, interpretations and descriptions, both realized and imagined. If, as Bruner states, "Narrative "truth" is judged by its verisimilitude rather than its verifiability", then truth and fact may be stratified (1991, p. 13).

Blatner suggests a postmodern approach to dispelling the notion of absolute truth makes way for creative expression through personal narrative (1997). Nevertheless, there are still important distinctions to be made between fact and fiction. According to

Schaeffer, one important quality to consider is whether narrative inquiry advances claims of truth in *reference* to fact, relevance or credibility, whereas fictional narrative does not necessarily posit any such claim (Schaeffer, 2013). Bruner does not draw such distinct lines in the sand (1991). Bruner insists that life-writing "is an extension of fiction, rather than the reverse, that the shape of life comes first from imagination rather than from experience" (The Autobiographical Process, 1995, p. 176).

If a positive correlation exists between original and *unresolved* trauma and secondary victimization, it will follow that a similar correlation would exist between *recovery* from trauma and the ability of adults to gain control and prevent secondary victimization. When personal disclosure in narrative is part of the recovery process (Pennebaker, 1995) our collective social responsibility to victims should require that we consider what is in a victim's best interest when assuming a stance on how their truth is told. If fictionalizing allows the important or difficult truth to be told, then the decision about writing the story as creative non-fiction should uphold the greater needs of the writer. Obviously, this is not the case when a victim is preparing a Victim Impact Statement to be used within the justice process. Nevertheless, stories of pain, suffering and oppression may lead to the secondary victimization of the author when they are harshly scrutinized by legal questions interested solely in establishing truth and fact and the chronology of events.

There is a legitimate concern that harsh scrutiny and judgement will silence the disclosure of important and difficult knowledge rather than to reliably satisfy questions of truth that can lead to deeper insights and understanding of victims of childhood maltreatment. Moreover, disclosure is an important part of the recovery process for some trauma victims. The collective social responsibility to victims of maltreatment should be informed by the awareness that harsh social judgments can lead to their secondary victimization and compel us to consider what is in the victim's best interest when it comes to how their truth is told. Creative non-fiction is an appropriate genre for expression of trauma stories for many and, in fact, could be the only way for some victims to tell the important and difficult truth of their personal experience. Academic discussion of autoethnography as genre and methodology and the development of the theory should not advance at the expense of authentic voice for the tellers of personal stories.

Narrative accounts of personal life experiences can be equally therapeutic to the author whether they are written or produced as factual representations, or creative expressions such as personal mythology that involves the narrative use of sub-selves or through the creation of fictional characters. The important elements of truth can be multidimensional and dependent on personal epistemology for both the storyteller and the audience. The value of fictionalized disclosure notwithstanding, having the ability to tell ones' story as an expression of personal truth should not be underestimated.

Bruner suggests one valid objective in writing the *self* is "the 'awakening' out of a frozen narrative about an author's personal life in order to risk forging a new one, a migration of identity" (1995, p. 162). The writing of *self* is a matter of personification of personal experiences that have taken place in a time and place other than now. This personification generates a metaphor for self that is a composite construct of memories, meanings, interpretations and understandings of previous choices and actions taken, informed by individual experiences within the context of personal culture. As such, it can be argued that this written *self* is at all times a fabrication and manifestation of creative meaning-making.

Personal Mythology and Poetry

The story titled *The Legend* is an example of personal mythology that makes use of the anthropomorphized characters of wolves in the wilderness (Fox, The Write to Justice, 2014, p. 261). This writing was primarily an exercise in the creation of a fictionalized vision of reconciliation between a mother and daughter. While I did not experience a great deal of satisfaction in the writing process, in that it was not based on a feeling discourse reflective of my emotional state at the time it was written, I was able to express a context I felt was missing in the writing in earlier chapters. The wilderness and the description of seasonal changes allowed me to place the protagonist into the context of the cyclical nature of change and the circumstances over which we have no control. The final encounter between mother and daughter, despite a history of injury and abandonment, was peaceful. Both were able to recognize their connection to one another from another time and move on in their individual life cycles. The final scene represents a feeling of peace and letting go. Having the freedom to explore genres such as poetry and creative non-fiction was liberating. It opened a window that enabled the expression of emotion and lived experience that was impossible for me otherwise. The following excerpt exemplifies the powerful impact of expressive writing on the meaning-making process for me as the writer.

> I wanted to claim my right to say *I am here.*
>
> I wanted to say *I was hurt and while I understand there were circumstances that influenced many of those hurts, the fact remains there was a great injury.*
>
> I wanted to say *it matters when you destroy the hope in a child. It matters when you injure a child. It matters when it happens to any child. So, it also matters that it happened to me.*
>
> I was the child who was left behind. (Fox, The Write to Justice, 2014, pp. 208-209)

Through autoethnography, I was, in effect, bearing witness to my own recollections as reconstructed memories (Frank, 2013, pp. Kindle Locations 2178-2179). Shifting between the perspectives of a child and an adult and giving expression through a feeling discourse impacted *the way I understood* the ways I have been deeply affected by traumatic abuse but more, it allowed me to move beyond being the victim. The "thick description" (Ellis C. A., 2011, p. 5) calls on you, the reader, to have a compassionate, affective response to the suffering described in the text that is representative of childhood victimization.

6. Victim Narratives and Therapeutic Justice

In the discussion of the impact of trauma and crime on victims, this chapter evaluates the benefits and shortcomings of Victim Impact Statements as an opportunity for expression by victims of crime and explores how the current practice fails to address problems associated with loss of voice. I conclude with a list of recommendations for victim writing in the context of therapeutic and restorative justice that are best implemented through victims' services and supports, without compromising the needs or processes of the justice system.

Historical Justification for Inclusion of Victim Impact Statements

In a comprehensive review of the function and purpose of Victim Impact Statements (VIS), Roberts and Erez (2004) take the position that the original intent of victim narratives was for the expressive and communicative value, but this was subsequently replaced by an impact model that stressed the impact of a crime on the victim should be considered in the context of sentencing. They further posit that the impact model overlays with Roach's punitive model of victim participation (as cited by Roberts & Erez, 2004), where the communicative and expressive functions model interfaces with restorative justice principles. Roach argues that the punitive model of victim participation is adversarial, where the rights and needs of the victim are seemingly "pitted against" (p. 29) the rights of the accused (Roach, 1999).

According to Roberts and Erez (2004), current impact based Court procedures seldom create an opportunity for victims to tell their stories about the way a crime has affected them, using their own words to do so. Often, the Victim Impact Statement is written in answer to carefully-constructed questions that omit any references the Court finds inflammatory or inappropriate to sentencing decisions, effectively silencing the victim's own voice. Moreover, these predetermined questions fail to support an individual's need for self-expression in ways that could promote recovery from the trauma or crime they have experienced (Roberts & Erez, 2004). This restriction on language and expression can be challenging and frustrating for victims. In fact, some victims experience a form of secondary victimization and social injury when they feel their needs are not treated sensitively or that they are not receiving the supports they require (Algonquin College, 2013). A more sensitive approach to how victims are supported as they write these important life experiences can help prevent this particular form of re-victimization by the current system and practice.

Therapeutic Jurisprudence, Restorative Justice and Victim Narratives

A theory of therapeutic or restorative jurisprudence argues that legal procedures, rules and those involved in the justice process become social forces that are sometimes beneficial and sometimes anti-therapeutic (Wexler, 2008). The National Justice Institute (Goldberg, 2011) embraces the concept of therapeutic justice as a 'problem-solving approach' to the law in action. Restorative justice measures strongly emphasize victim participation and a victim's ability to speak freely (Goldberg, 2011). According to Goldberg, restorative justice "may reduce post traumatic stress among victims, and have a positive impact on the physical and psychological health of victims and offenders" (2011, p. B18). Victim statements are an important part of that process. One survey of victims in the Province of Quebec determined that although most victims said they had prepared a VIS, the process is not currently satisfying their needs for recognition and participation in the criminal justice process (Wemmers, 2008).

Victims' service workers attempt to safeguard the VIS against language that appears to compete with an offender's right to due process in order to preserve its admissibility to the Court. However, we have missed an opportunity for meaningful disclosure of a difficult life experience in a way that can promote recovery for some victims (Pennebaker J. W., 1995).

The Impact of Criminal Victimization on Victims

According to the General Survey of statistics collected in 2009, there were close to 1.6 million Canadians aged 15 years and over who reported having been the victim of sexual assault, a robbery or physical assault in the preceding 12 months (Statistics Canada, 2010). Physical assault was the most common form of violence, followed by sexual assault and robbery (Statistics Canada, 2010). The Canadian Centre for Justice Statistics reports that among those Canadians who reported having been victims of a crime in the 12 months preceding the survey, 38% said they had been victimized more than once. Of those, half were victimized twice while the other half were victimized three or more times (Perreault, 2004). According to Fortier et al., (2009)) re-victimization for victims of childhood sexual abuse in particular, can exacerbate existing symptoms of trauma and strain adaptive coping mechanisms, often leading to avoidance as a coping mechanism. Significantly, this strain affects information processing and risk assessment in future scenarios when symptoms of Post-Traumatic Stress Disorder are present. Symptoms of strain adaptive coping mechanisms also include substance abuse and other high risk behaviors such as prostitution (Fortier, et al., 2009).

At the same time, many victims demonstrate resilience and are able to recover with an ability to move forward. Some will, however, find it more challenging to move forward and will be at risk for development of Post-Traumatic Stress Disorder and Acute

Stress Disorder (Hill, 2009). One of the reasons that trauma and crime is so devastating is that it reveals our vulnerability, undermining our sense of control over our lives. Victims need to be heard if they are to experience restoration of power, which is necessary for psychological wholeness (Algonquin College, 2013). It is important to establish training pedagogy for victim services workers that will sensitize them to victim writing as a function of self-expression and instill awareness of creative life writing processes (Hunt, Autobiography and the Psychotherapeutic Process, 1998). Education can guide workers who facilitate a life writing process and create awareness of when referrals should be made to counsellors.

Compassion and Social Justice

Worldwide, the formation of truth and reconciliation commissions signify another trend in restorative justice. The Archbishop Desmond Tutu describes the African principle of *Ubuntu,* which broadly recognizes that the humanity of one is inextricably bound to the humanity of another (2000). As governments have established Truth and Reconciliation Commissions globally, to attempt to address horrible wrongs such as genocide, apartheid, atrocities in war and more, there is an interest in fostering reconciliation and hope for forgiveness. The foundation of this process is the creation of an opportunity for the stories of victims and offenders alike *to be told openly and heard with compassion.* Tutu himself describes his incredible difficulty in hearing

74

tens of thousands of narratives from people expressing the horrors they had survived, as well as stories about those who had not survived. He describes the terrible pain expressed by those who had *committed* some of the worst crimes against humanity. After sitting on the *Commission for Truth and Reconciliation* in South Africa and hearing testimonials for eighteen months from people who described suffering, torture, anguish and devastation under apartheid, Tutu wrote his account of the process in his book *"No Future Without Forgiveness."*

Similar opportunities seldom exist for individual victims within the Canadian Justice System. There are provisions that allow victims of crime to prepare a narrative description of their experiences as Victim Impact Statements, however, many victims have expressed dissatisfaction with the restrictions placed on how their stories must be told, leaving them feeling a sense of 'loss of voice.' Victims of childhood maltreatment are often not able to fully disclose their story at the time an incident occurs. Often their stories are not disclosed until many years later. Moreover, some forms of childhood victimization may not be considered a crime or have been dealt with by social responses other than the criminal justice system such as child welfare agencies. These victims' stories are often documented and interpreted by agencies and third parties when the victim is a minor. It is unlikely any formal process of written disclosure will involve the victim directly. Nevertheless, life-writing can be a powerful and important part of the healing and recovery process. Life-writing as a process is concerned with more than relating historical facts and events. It is a reflective process concerned with creating meaning-making and understanding of lived experience. While victims are usually advised that they are able to write a Victim Impact Statement (VIS), they often feel unheard in the justice process even when they do so. There is little sense of interaction between the victim and the larger justice system once the victim's story has been submitted, at times contributing to a deeper sense of invisibility.

One exception in Canadian law, on paper at any rate, is the hearing process offered by the Ontario Criminal Injuries Compensation Board. Victims of crime – by a fairly broad definition – are entitled to request a hearing whereby they can present their story. This system of justice for victims does not depend on the criminal conviction of an offender or successful prosecution of a crime to proceed (Government of Ontario, 2013). However, in a scathing report by the Ontario Ombudsman called *Investigation into the Treatment of Victims by the Criminal Injuries Compensation Board: "Adding Insult to Injury"* (2007), the Office of the Ombudsman insists victims are still not being heard. André Marin describes an agonizing reality that often results in further damage to victims.

> It takes, on average, three years for an application to be processed. Of those applications that are received – approximately 4,000 to 5,000 per year – the Criminal

Injuries Compensation Board succeeds in adjudicating, on average, only 2,500 per year. The Attorney General has predicted that by October 2007, there will be 17,500 backlogged compensation claims worth $109 million. The Board depends, shamefully, on attrition as well. Approximately half of those who attempt to file claims are so overwhelmed by the Board's complex documentation and process-based demands that they give up. …These applicants are not helped when they flounder, but left to fail. This report chronicles an embarrassing series of hurdles placed in the path of vulnerable victims of violent crime (Ontario Ombudsman, 2007).

Victims of crime are already marginalized by their lack of active participation and visibility in the traditional justice system. Much work lies ahead if we intend to include their stories in a meaningful way as part of our social experience. The process of applying for permission to submit an application for a hearing is described in Chapter 20 in *The Write to Justice* (Fox 2014). However, after permission was granted to proceed with the application, the decision was made to not move forward with seeking compensation via this process.

7. Research and Applied Ethics

When I began the writing process, it did not occur to me that fiction or imaginative works (creating composite characters and events to tell a story that did not bear my own name, my own life events) could serve my needs. I reflected extensively on the implications of using my name, rather than to write anonymously, and the implications of identifying others with whom I had close or even distance relationships. I *felt* there was no point to telling the story, to my personal disclosure if I failed to use real names, real people and real events. However, 'feeling' this was not enough. I needed to consider my decision in the context of the purpose I hoped to serve by disclosing these personal identifiers:

> It would never be enough just to expose what was wrong, although it would bring some sense of relief and perhaps closure. Exposing injury and injustice was more than just a matter of creating a public record. Truth is more than just an abstract concept or a subjective acceptance of the chronology of events. It is about our perception and understanding of humanity and our individuality – our *personhood*. I began to realize forgiveness was not necessarily a destination spot one could arrive at and just stay forever. There was a continuum of events necessary to make that journey, and while it was my responsibility to move forward with my own healing, it was not a journey that should, or even could happen in isolation. I had lived in isolation and

silence. That was part of the problem, not the solution (Fox, The Write to Justice, 2014, pp. 212-213).

Ellis concludes in her article *Telling Secrets, Revealing Lives: Relational Ethics in Research with Intimate Others* by saying:

> As researchers, we long to do ethical research that makes a difference. To come close to these goals, we constantly have to consider which questions to ask, which secrets to keep, and which truths are worth telling (Ellis C. , 2007, p. 26).

I made the decision to name my mother, as well as certain others according to the following criteria. These concerns were reconciled, in part, in the context of guidelines suggested by Etherington (2004, p. 148). These serve as the criteria for review of autoethnographic writings for publication.

a) *What is the impact of this work on me?* I had to reconcile the ethical challenges to making decisions about subject names, anonymity and relational ethics (Etherington, 2004, p. 148). I had spent decades feeling invisible. Naming the (alleged) abusers, as well as describing the harm I experienced was my right as a victim. While there is no official Statute of Limitations in Canada, in truth there was no process available to me so many years later through a criminal process. I had named my mother in my official application to the Ontario Criminal Injuries Compensation Board and this was now a matter of public record. The relationship with my mother is *primal* and my identity is intrinsically bound to her. In naming myself I inevitably named my mother if I was to tell my story at all. I made the decision to do so boldly and with courage.

b) *What is the impact of this work on others?* Naming the abusers had to contribute something positive beyond my own need to expose the harm. Certainly, I could expect that there would be a risk to my mother, psychologically, socially, perhaps legally and even physically. The positive contribution of publicly sharing my own truth, shared through the process of autoethnography, is that it is representative of my culture of survivors. However, it has a value that is not easily quantified. I felt I had an ethical obligation to speak that truth. Otherwise, I was merely perpetuating a cycle of secrecy, silence and harm with no hope for reconciliation. My silence served only to protect the abusers.

There were consequences to my decision to publish.

Purposive Writing

My experience in the past with disclosure of my experience of childhood victimization, was that many people felt overwhelming discomfort at the idea of a child experiencing abuse at the hands of her mother and made it clear that their preference was to not know the details of experiences like mine. The gender stereotypes about women were inconsistent with the reality that women *are* capable of violence, including violence against children. The perception of women as nurturers and as victims of domestic violence, as well as awareness of the power dynamics that create vulnerability, did not easily accommodate an understanding of women as abusers who act with agency. It is a legitimate conclusion that the dynamic of vulnerability creates a context of oppression that can be subsequently expressed through aggression and violence as suggested by Shaw and Dubois:

> For feminists in particular, the issue of women's violence
> has been difficult to come to terms with. Since the focus of
> public and academic attention tends, as always, to fall upon
> murder, much of the discourse and literature about
> women's use of violence over the past 15 years has been
> concerned with women in abusive relationships who kill
> their abuser. Thus women's violence has been framed
> largely as a response to an abusive situation or past abusive

experiences (Understanding Violence By Women: A Review of the Literature: Introduction, 1995, p. np).

As a researcher, I struggled to feel that autoethnography and my own personal story had academic value. I understood that the process of writing in a personal voice (subjectively) in order to tell my story had a purpose beyond my own edification. While the writing did have personal therapeutic value, the purpose of the research was also to be heard and to be understood socially by others, who would serve as a witness to my own lived experience and the experiences of other victims. Ellis discusses the importance of reaching others through autoethnography:

> ... the autoethnographer not only tries to make personal experience meaningful and cultural experience engaging, but also, by producing accessible texts, she or he may be able to reach wider and more diverse mass audiences that traditional research usually disregards, a move that can make personal and social change possible for more people. (Ellis, 2011, p. 5)

Etherington suggests that ethical decisions about the research and writing process, what to disclose, whom to identify and even genre, is influenced by the intended purpose of the writing (2004, p. 146). The initial purpose or focus of the research can change as the process is undertaken. Nevertheless, remaining focused on our main purpose (Etherington, 2004, p. 148/286) helps to prevent diversions of intention that leads to the problem of narcissistic writing that Leon Anderson is so concerned with (2006, p. 386). The responsibility for recollection is complicated when the subject is *self*, and because those recollections implicate relational others, it becomes even more so. Some researchers are satisfied with the therapeutic experience that the process of autoethnography provides and have no intention of publishing their work in the public domain. They edit or omit any material that is potentially harmful to others. However, one should assume there is always the potential for any subject to read the account of their lives presented in the research text. When the researcher hopes or intends to publish, the decision to disclose the written account that includes representation of others can result in complex relational challenges. Ellis characterizes this as potentially opening up "a Pandora's box of communication complications" (2007, p. 17). There are times when identifying information can harm relational others, or harm the researcher/subject of the writing. One possibility for harm prevention is the decision to not publish in the public domain, although Redl cautions that in research, inclusion of identifying information in any document, submitted to an institution does constitute publication (Redl, *Instructor Notes*, 2014). Another possibility is to publish using a researcher pseudonym and to make whatever changes are necessary to protect the identity of relational others. Even so, this is not always successful (Ellis C. , 2007, p. np). The scope of the research, the location of the events and the experiences described along with other salient features of the story can all serve to identify the subjects. It should be noted that there is also the potential for making erroneous conclusions about the identity of subjects leading to the incorrect attribution of certain actions to the 'wrong' person. The inclusion of others requires special, ethical considerations (Anderson L. , 2006). Having reflected upon my own process of writing autoethnography, these ethical considerations posed the most significant challenges.

Ethical Problems with Identifying Subjects

Reflexivity is an integral part of the process of qualitative research: it is, as well, a critical element of autoethnographic writing. Reflexivity is a critical process if a researcher is to gain insight into his or her own thoughts, feelings, beliefs and biases (Rivas, 2013, p. 499). When a researcher decides to include and disclose elements of a subject's lived experience, the potential impact on that person must be carefully considered.

Ellis reflects on the ethical decisions a researcher makes that can impact subjects and describes three dimensions to consider. The first dimension is one of informed consent and procedures that protect "confidentiality, rights to privacy, deception, and protecting human subjects from harm" (Ellis C. , 2007, p. 4). The second dimension concerns problems that arise in the field or within some aspect of the process of doing autoethnography. Ellis cites problems such as when a subject "discloses something harmful, asks for help, or voices discomfort with a question or her or his own response" (p. 4). The third dimension of relational ethics has no set rules of practice and is essentially grounded in an ethic of dignity and respect for those with whom a researcher has an intimate relationship (p. 4). Researchers implicate others with their work, sometimes directly and sometimes indirectly and often in unintended and unanticipated ways (Ellis C. A., 2011). The autoethnographer must carefully balance decisions to "protect the privacy and safety of others by altering identifying characteristics such as circumstance, topics discussed, or characteristics like race, gender, name, place, or appearance (in) ethnography, the relationships with others" in order to meet ethical commitments (Ellis C. A., 2011, p. 9).

The dilemma of whether to use the subject's real name when sharing memories is often complicated, even when the subject is the researcher *self*. Frank begins his own assessment of ethical considerations in *The Wounded Storyteller*, saying, "the self-story is never just a *self*-story but becomes a self/*other*-story" (2013, Kindle Locations 2151-2152). There is an important intersection of voice, memory and responsibility when a story is told, such that in order to find the subjective voice, one must first take responsibility for the memories that are shared with (and about – *my emphasis*) others. According to his *Ethic of Recollection*, sharing memories creates an important "moral opportunity to set right what was done wrong or incompletely" (Kindle Locations 2157-2158) in the past. This opportunity is realized, in part, by giving memories a context of time and place which helps create a *then* and *now* perspective (Frank, 2013).

> Voice is found in the recollection of memories. The storyteller's responsibility is to witness the memory of what happened, and to set this memory right by providing a better example for others to follow (Frank, 2013, pp. Kindle Locations 2178-2179)

In relation to the risk of harm to the researcher when the subject is *self*, Etherington discusses some of the implications of bias encountered by researchers who have disclosed their own stories, where they are seemingly pathologized by their peers in the academic community and their career suffers later (2004, p. 141). This is not a bias with negative consequences for all researchers. In fact, Ellis describes a student who she had particular concern for when she wrote of her own suicide attempt:

> I tell them they have to live in the world of those they write about and those they write for and to. I tell them they must be careful how they present themselves. "Writing about your depression and suicide attempt while taking sick leave and trying to earn tenure?" I ask, aghast, and the former student replies, "Yes, I have to write myself out of my depression." She does, and gets a teaching award the next year (Jago, 2002) (Ellis C. , 2007, p. 25).

My personal experience with bias is complex. In some respects, I believe my career and public persona as a professional suffered as my childhood victimization was publicized. I became viewed as a 'broken' person with a complex psychological history. My personal and professional judgements and conclusions were open to scrutiny based on the perception that my story and the impact of childhood victimization was made public. At times, this seemed fair and relevant if I was, upon reflection, prepared to acknowledge my own personal biases and the challenges I faced as a survivor. At other times, an assessment by others seemed unfair and incomplete in analysis and more a reflection of their personal context of understanding.

Privacy, Confidentiality and Protection From Harm

The original objectives leading to my decision to publish my life story required the disclosure of identifying information that had the potential to harm others if I proceeded with naming my abuser. I moved forward with this risk to others in mind and in balance felt it was critical to avoid fictionalizing the writing. In order to mitigate the potential for harm, I took the following steps:

1. I informed as many of the subjects as possible that I intended to identify them, prior to publishing the book

and invited their comments and their wishes with respect to my intentions.

2. I encouraged subjects, where possible, to consider the potential repercussions to being identified.

3. I asked subjects to review what I had written prior to publishing, unless to do so represented any sense of real danger to myself or others.

4. I sent copies of the book in draft form by registered mail to subjects when and where possible. The mailing of the draft included named professionals and others.

5. Specifically, I sent a copy of the book to my mother and father by special delivery mail. The copy sent to my parents was the only copy that was sent back to me by return mail. I have no knowledge of whether they read the book prior to returning it to me, or not.

8. Healing and Recovery

Despite the current deficiencies in the justice system, victim writing and disclosure of a traumatic event can be therapeutic. Early research by Pennebaker referred to as the *Confession Studies,* reported subjective findings of improved health and well-being for the subjects (Pennebaker J. , 1997 Revised). The results were significant enough to warrant a subsequent collaborative effort between Pennebaker, Kiecolt-Glaser, and Glaser in 1988 (Pennebaker J. , 1997 Revised, p. 35). Research findings concluded that 4 consecutive sessions of 15-25 minutes of narrative writing will accomplish powerful changes when a difficult personal experience is expressed. Moreover, there is evidence that the benefits of narrative writing go beyond subjective experience to include certain measures of stress reduction, immunological activity and general well-being. These benefits may be attributed to the cathartic value of expressing emotions attached to the event, or based on certain insights gained in the process (Pennebaker J. , 1997 Revised).

Narrative writing appears to be most beneficial when the author goes beyond simply recounting events that took place in the past, such as describing a traumatic incident. The real benefit is in the evaluation of a function or effect of that incident on present life through the reflective process (Hunt C. , 1998, p. 187). Hunt recommends that a framework should be in place where there is interaction with anyone who serves as the facilitator or a narrative process. This could be a victim services worker, social worker, or a psychotherapist or professional counselor.

Religion and Spirituality Integrated With the Healing Process

The belief in a non-material or spiritual reality includes the possibility of a supreme being, the supernatural, life after death and belief in the complex space of existence we have come to know as 'spirituality.' Moreover, the acceptance of a non-material reality is dominant in North America and many individuals "describe spirituality as the most important source of strength and direction in their lives" (Millers, 1999, p. 5). In response to the perceived need for inclusion of spirituality in health care, the Province of Alberta, has developed a 50 page manual through Alberta Health Services titled *Health Care and Religious Beliefs*. The introductory foreword states:

> The current medical model in health and wellness acknowledges the treatment of an individual as a whole with a need to treat the bio/psycho/social aspects of health. A growing realization in health care is that this model also must acknowledge the spiritual health of an individual in order to maximize the healing and recovery process (Alberta Health Services, 2009)

This resource looks at the special needs, core beliefs and concerns of faith communities from the traditions of Aboriginal faith, Buddhism, Christian Science, Church of Jesus Christ of Latter-day Saints, Eastern Orthodoxy, Hindu faith, Islamic faith, Jehovah's Witnesses, Jewish faith, Protestantism, Roman Catholicism, Seventh-day Adventist, Sikh faith, United Church faith community as well as broader multicultural and interfaith perspectives (Alberta Health Services, 2009). When we examine the great religions of the world we find within them all a philosophy or perspective on the meaning of human suffering. In our predominantly Christian culture in North America, one common belief is that suffering serves the positive purpose of deepening one's spirituality. Religious faith can bring a perspective to suffering that offers comfort or strength to those who have experienced childhood trauma and maltreatment and throughout the process of recovery. Religious faith supports the hope for a future where the victim is not consumed with pain and despair (Fox, 2001).

Despite the predominance of spiritual belief and experiences that are shared among people from all academic, social and cultural backgrounds, talking openly about religiosity can provoke strong reactions from others. Among the most difficult of those reactions is that of a sceptic who challenges any claim to spiritual 'knowing' by virtue of how un-provable and personal those experiences, or the meaning attributed to them, can be. In fact, it is fair to say that many spiritual experiences represent a distinct form of 'difficult knowledge' precisely because they are met with such broad social scepticism.

Patricia Pearson became fascinated with the social stigma that seemingly restricts open discussion of spiritual experiences with the dying and their bereaved in her book *Opening Heaven's Door – What the dying may be trying to tell us about where they're going* (2014). She gives many examples of research studies and stories told by nurses and other people who work with the dying and their grieving families that confirm how common spiritual experiences are for most people. Moreover, there appears to be a collective taboo imposed on open discussion of spiritual experiences without having them simply dismissed as hallucinations or delusions. This creates a context for these mysterious explorations that limits our ability to talk about them and prevents us from developing a deeper understanding of non-material existence (2014, pp. Ch. 2 10-12 of 37). According to Pearson's research, half of the population around the world, and in some cultures even more, have spiritual experiences that are mysterious and not easily reconciled to the scientific model applied as the gold standard of evidence that such events are plausible, and can be explained satisfactorily.

When a sense of the spiritual gives strength and comfort and helps to create a context and sense of meaning for individuals, we must not limit the expression of spiritual experience. Where social taboo creates a culture of disapproval and scepticism, it is especially difficult for individuals who have experienced childhood

92

victimization to share their experiences openly. Sharing of personal experiences, even experiences viewed as positive and sacred, can be a sensitive issue for people who have often been groomed by offenders to keep silent about the abuse they suffer. The consequences of disclosure can be perceived as high risk for victims. It is important to honour the experiences that give victims (and others) a sense of comfort and strength, especially when spiritual experiences are so deeply intimate.

When we consider how the appraisal or meaning-making process is the most relevant indicator of victim outcome according to the research by Martin as discussed earlier (Martin, 2013 as cited on p. 12), it seems likely that spirituality and religion have the potential to facilitate victim recovery by contributing an "important source of strength and direction" (Millers, 1999, p. 5).

Forgiveness

The subject of forgiveness is difficult for many victims and survivors. Forgiveness is the subject of considerable research today. What is of utmost concern to many victims is the reason for choosing forgiveness as part of the healing and recovery process. In the 2014 publication by Archbishop Desmond Tutu, winner of the Nobel Peace Prize in 1984, and his daughter Reverend Mpho Tutu, titled *The Book of Forgiving – The Fourfold Path for Healing Ourselves and Our World*, the authors list the important reasons for forgiving:

- Forgiveness is beneficial to our health.

- Forgiveness offers freedom from the past, from a perpetrator, from future victimization.

- Forgiveness heals families and communities.

- We forgive so we don't suffer, physically or mentally, the corrosive effects of holding on to anger and resentment.

- We are all interconnected and have a shared humanity.

- Forgiveness is a gift we give to ourselves (Tutu & Tutu, 2014, pp. Kindle Locations 319-323).

Despite these compelling reasons to consciously forgive a person who has harmed us, forgiveness requires four (according to Tutu & Tutu) distinct parts in the process. What are most relevant to this paper are Steps One and Two of the Fourfold Path. They are: Telling the Story and Naming the Hurt (Tutu & Tutu, 2014, pp. Kindle Locations 74-75).

Prior to writing my story in autoethnography, when I approached the idea of forgiveness throughout the years, I felt as though I was being pushed by others to forgive something that I had never named. I felt I was being asked to forgive my mother and others, but in the absence of my ability to tell my story and name the hurt, I made little progress. I describe the meaning I attributed to my feelings about forgiveness as follows:

> I read everything I could get my hands on about forgiveness but kept hitting a wall. Most of what was out there made sense to me, but I felt like it kept jumping to the end of the story without really getting to the heart of the process. I started to feel like either the problem was with me and my inability or reluctance to get to forgiveness. Either that or what I meant by forgiveness and what many others meant were not the same thing (Fox, The Write to Justice, 2014, p. 209).

I knew my mother did not have the *intention* of malice at the heart of her crimes against my person. I did have feelings of empathy, compassion and understanding for her humanity and the context of her actions. Nevertheless, this was not the same as forgiveness that could only come about through speaking my own truth, telling the story and naming the hurt. It was imperative that I give my own meaning to my experiences and to the question of forgiveness.

Empowering the Voices of Victims

In Canada, a theory of law embedded in values of therapeutic jurisprudence argues for acknowledgment that legal procedures and rules and those actors involved such as lawyers and judges, become social forces of law in action (Wexler, 2008). In Canadian jurisprudence, the concept of therapeutic justice is embraced as a 'problem-solving approach' that strongly emphasizes victim participation (Goldberg, 2011). According to Goldberg, restorative justice "may reduce posttraumatic stress among victims, and have a positive impact on the physical and psychological health of victims and offenders" (2011, p. B18). Victim statements are considered an important part of that process. The principle of therapeutic jurisprudence calls for research that helps to reduce the anti-therapeutic effects of the justice process while enhancing those that are therapeutic without compromise to other values and processes of law (Wemmers, 2008).

The Canadian Resource Centre for Victims of Crime *Statement on the Impact of Victimization* (2006) agrees that victims need to be able to express their emotions and tell their stories. Victims often need to have their experiences validated and have their story heard by a nonjudgmental listener. Even a group setting outside of the courtroom can provide a safe and supportive environment for victims to both tell their stories and to be heard (2006). Victim narratives and disclosure of a traumatic event can be therapeutic. Early research by Pennebaker referred to as the *Confession Studies* evaluated data collected through the self-reporting of participants (1997 Revised). The subjective findings of improved health and well-being were significant enough to warrant a collaborative effort between Pennebaker, Kiecolt-Glaser, and Glaser in 1988 (Pennebaker, 1997 Revised, p. 35). Pennebaker's research findings concluded that 4 consecutive sessions of 15-25 minutes of narrative writing will accomplish powerful changes when a difficult personal experience is expressed. Further, there is evidence that the benefits of narrative writing go beyond subjective experience to include quantifiable measures of physiological stress reduction. Pennebaker's model could be implemented as an initial part of the process of victims' services workers helping victims to prepare their narratives by first affording them the opportunity to express fully, in their own words, disclosure of the traumatic event. By prioritizing the victim's needs for expression, communication and disclosure can be accommodated without compromise to the final, officially submitted Victim Impact Statement.

Challenges and Problems

Despite the empirical evidence that supports the position that a therapeutic approach to writing is beneficial for victims, there is a lingering opposition by some theorists to the development of practical and pedagogical applications. One concern stems from problems with the lack of preparedness on the part of victim service workers and others to deal with the crisis that can arise when narrative inquiry opens the flood gates to deeper, unresolved and disturbing emotions. The potential for emotional crisis is of particular concern, and perhaps more likely, where there is a history of previous victimizations such as childhood sexual abuse (Fortier, et al., 2009). It is important that some amount of training in narrative writing be made available for facilitators of victim narrative processes. Training should include a familiarity with narrative writing processes and should sensitize the facilitator to the potential for problems when disturbing emotions and thoughts surface for victims. There should be adequate access to resource information for referral to mental health professionals, especially those familiar with narrative psychotherapeutic technique, if required by participants (Bracher, 1999). Bracher posits that regardless of whether writing is academic, psychoanalytic or as an exploration of social problems toward change, conflicts of a pedagogical, personal or social nature can be explored and resolved in a positive way through narrative writing. There is a potential for problems to arise if the instructor or facilitator is insensitive to a power dynamic that could push an individual to enter into disturbing thoughts and feelings at a pace that is not self-determined. Bracher counters these concerns by insisting that when the pace is self-determined, psychoanalytic writing is likely to be a fail-safe process (Bracher, 1999).

There are instances where writing can be problematic and according to Pennebaker, there are times when there is a "downside of writing" (1990). For instance, when the process is little more than an indulgence in anger and the writing is only an opportunity to vent, writers may find themselves feeling more angry and frustrated if their writing is not accompanied by a process of reflection and resolution. Similarly, writing that is focused on someone other than *self* can exacerbate feelings of distress and fail to bring about resolution of troublesome feelings (p. 204). Where victims are expressing harm that was experienced by offenders it is important to be aware of how healing and recovery can be impacted by this type of writing. The reflective process can be equally emotional and intellectual. Pennebaker cautions that writing focusing on intellectual insights into *self* and the behaviours of others is unlikely to have the desired result (1990, pp. 202-203). It is the reflective process that allows one to write with feeling and to explore emotions that is likely to provide therapeutic benefit.

Both Pennebaker (1990) and Anderson (2006) discuss potential problems with narcissistic writing and self-absorption. Deep, personal reflection can be uniquely beneficial in the interest of personal growth and development but it takes place in relative isolation from others. Pennebaker points out that reflective writing does not provide opportunities for meaningful, and reciprocal interactions with others (1990, p. 204). Writing can provide a type of insulation that actually prevents growth if the writer does not take the actions necessary in order to have a meaningful life. Making changes can be difficult and the therapeutic narrative process is necessarily one that facilitates positive strategies for taking action.

9. Conclusion

Autoethnography as a qualitative research methodology produces data suitable for meta-analysis when the interest is in gaining insight into the lived experience of childhood victimization and the relevant cultural, social, historical and political context of individual experience. As the researcher self, the mapping and creation of an inventory of social, political and cultural influences created a terrain of context that allowed me to reflect on and make meaning of the complex life of my mother as a woman born in the 1950s who conceived a child outside of the conventions of marriage, and her subsequent actions. The contextual stressors are significant for the mother and the possible development of postpartum mental disorder after the birth of her baby girl that are causal to the subsequent violence, maltreatment and harm inflicted by a mother on her daughter. Through the process of autoethnography where the researcher *self* is the subject, the author provides a thick description of embodied experience and meaning-making, as part of the process of recovery and toward sensitizing the reader. This phenomenological approach to research methodology addresses concerns with researcher subjectivity and bias and agrees with the notion that subjective experience is grounded in self-experience (Anderson L. , 2006). Nevertheless, autoethnography reaches beyond the subjective experience of *self* to include the larger social world. Phenomenological research provides information that can be broadly applied to a population that has experienced the phenomenon of interest. The person who has experienced the phenomenon of interest, even when that person is the researcher *self*, is representative of that population such that their experience can be applied to developing nomothetic understandings of social processes.

The research question asks, is creative non-fiction in autoethnography a productive qualitative research methodology for the study of the lived experience of childhood victimization, leading to a deeper understanding of this complex social problem? Can narrative expression through life-writing and creative non-fiction support the process of meaning-making for childhood victims? Where the question of productivity is assessed from an interdisciplinary perspective to determine how life-writing can support healing and recovery for victims of childhood maltreatment, the poststructuralist approach to contextualized meaning-making is consistent with autoethnography as methodology.

The question is un-concerned with establishing the accuracy of facts claimed in the description of embodied experience. We take, at face value, the veracity of claims made based on thick description of childhood victimization and maltreatment. In the interest of disclosure for therapeutic resolution and in order to establish the verisimilitude of the story, it is important to recognize that writing the *self* is a matter of *personification* of personal experiences that have taken place in a time and place other than now – in memory.

Writing creates a personification of experience as a metaphor for *self*. This is a composite construct of embodied experience and meanings, interpretations and understandings of previous events, informed by individual experiences within the context of personal culture. As such, it can be argued that this written *self* is at all times a fabrication and manifestation of creative meaning-making. The benefits of disclosure through life-writing appear to be significant whether or not the content is a work of creative non-fiction. In fact, the author of life-writing as creative non-fiction is more likely to suffer where there are influences by those in hierarchical positions who require the content and form of the writing to be other than what is determined by the author and disclosed according to their own pace and needs. These hierarchical positions can include therapists, legal writers or those with academic authority.

In the process of meaning-making the author explores the effects of traumatic abuse in a personal, social and cultural context. Important ethical considerations encountered through the decision making process whereby the decision to name the (alleged) perpetrator of childhood victimization were made on the basis of balancing the victim's need (my need) to name their abuser as an inalienable right of personhood with the need to protect others from harm. In essence, *The Write to Justice* (Fox, 2014) is a statement of truth and reconciliation for the victim. The identities of some individuals were changed in order to protect them from potential harm and where disclosure of their names was irrelevant to the purposive objectives of the writing, namely: to write in the interest of telling the story and naming the hurt, to provide a thick description of childhood victimization and maltreatment, and to produce an aesthetic text which calls on the reader to have a compassionate, affective response to the experience of childhood maltreatment and the subsequent process of healing and recovery (Ellis C. A., 2011, p. 5).

If the societal response to victims of childhood maltreatment and harm is to provide support and to change the way we operationalize victims' supports and services, we must be prepared to consider the authority of victims to tell their stories and identify their needs. The principles of Restorative Justice are significant to the way we identify and prioritize the needs of victims in their quest for healing and recovery. In addition to solutions available to victims within the justice systems, there are multiple pathways that we can implement toward fostering resilience in children and adults that can positively impact the ability to move on after trauma and harm, regardless of the type or degree of victimization experienced. As we explore optimal ways in which to provide support and to be innovative in the ways we operationalize victims' supports and services, we must be prepared to consider the authority of victims to tell their stories at their own pace and to identify their needs. The single most important determinant in positive victim outcome is the ability to make appraisals of traumatic events that include ways of understanding what occurred within the context of cultural, historical, political and other relevant adversities. Narrative disclosure of childhood maltreatment is an important part of the meaning-making process and expressive life-writing can be beneficial to many victims.

The number of children who are victimized in Canada is alarming. Restorative Justice Programs that utilize strategies in narrative expression and life-writing, including creative non-fiction, could be integrated with the current practice of Victim Offender mediation and traditional justice systems by making some innovative accommodations to the needs of victims. By responding to the needs of victims as a social justice imperative, we can implement meaningful practices that engage other actors capable of operationalizing change.

References

Administration on Children, Youth and Families. (2013). *Child Maltreatment 2012*. Maryland: Department of Health & Human Services.

Alberta Health Services. (2009). Health Care and Religious Beliefs. Calgary, Government of Alberta.

Algonquin College. (2013, November 27). *Statutory Development and Reform*. Retrieved from Victimization and the Law: Lesson 3: https://bbol.embanet.com/bbcswebdav/pid-789287-dt-content-rid-2410808_1/courses/AL-VIC0003/VIC0003/les3-2.htm

Algonquin College. (2013, November 27). *Victim-Related Provisions: Victim Impact Statements*. Retrieved from Victimization and the Law Lesson 8: Sentencing: https://bbol.embanet.com/bbcswebdav/pid-789287-dt-content-rid-2410808_1/courses/AL-VIC0003/VIC0003/les8-9.htm

Algonquin, B. e. (2004, 2006, 2007). *Resiliency*. Retrieved from Algonquin College - Victims of Crime Lesson Notes: https://bbol.embanet.com/bbcswebdav/pid-789248-dt-content-rid-2530043_1/courses/AL-VIC0002/VIC0002/les1-4.htm

Allison, D. (1992). *Bastard Out of Carolina*. New York: Dutton.

Anderson, E. (2012, September 21). *Feminist Epistemology and Philosophy of Science*. Retrieved from The Stanford Encyclopedia of Philosophy (Fall 2012 Edition): http://plato.stanford.edu/archives/fall2012/entries/feminism-epistemology/

Anderson, E. (2012, September 21). *Feminist Epistemology and Philosophy of Science*. Retrieved from The Stanford Encyclopedia of Philosophy (Fall 2012 Edition): http://plato.stanford.edu/archives/fall2012/entries/feminism-epistemology/

Anderson, L. (2006). Analytic Autoethnography. *Journal of Contemporary Ethnography 35:4*, 373-395.

Athabasca University E-Lab. (2013, September 25). *What is Digital Storytelling and How to Get Started*. Retrieved from Athabasca University E-Lab: https://elab.athabascau.ca/workshop/digital-storytelling

Blatner, A. (1997). The Implications of Postmodernism for Psychotherapy . *Individual Psychology, 53(4)*, 476-482.

Bracher, M. (1999). *The Writing Cure: Psychoanalysis, Composition, and the Aims of Education*. Carbondale: Southern Illinois University Press.

Bruner, J. (1991). The Narrative Construction of Reality. *Critical Inquiry 18 (Autumn 1991)* , 1-21.

Bruner, J. (1995). The Autobiographical Process. *Current Sociology 43.2* , 161-177.

Bryden, J. (2014, May 7). *Justin Trudeau says anti-abortion candidates can't run as Liberals.* Retrieved from National Post: http://news.nationalpost.com/2014/05/07/justin-trudeau-says-anti-abortion-candidates-cant-run-as-liberals/

Budani, D. M. (2007, September 13). *Culture and Language.* Retrieved from University of Delaware - Anthropology Department Dr. Budani Courses: www.udel.edu/anthro/budani/Culture%20and%20Language.pdf

Budani, D. M. (2009, January 28). *Language and Culture.* Retrieved from University of Delaware - Anthropology Department Dr. Budani Courses: http://www.udel.edu/anthro/budani/language.pdf

Butler, Judith, Scott, Joan W. (1992). *Contingent Foundations: Feminism and the Question of "Postmodernism" in Feminists Theorize the Political,* London & New York: Routledge

Calgary Communities Against Sexual Abuse . (2014, May 4). *Child Sexual Abuse Myths.* Retrieved from CCASA: http://www.calgarycasa.com/resources/child-sexual-abuse-myths/

Callanan, M. K. (2012). *Final Gifts: Understanding the Special Awareness, Needs, and Communications of the Dying (Kindle Edition).* Toronto: Simon & Schuster.

Canadian Resource Centre for Victims of Crime. (2006, October). *The Impact of Victimization.* Retrieved from Canadian Resource Centre for Victims of Crime: http://www.crcvc.ca/docs/victimization.pdf

Carvajal, A. (2008, Winter). *Sentencing in Canadian Law.* Retrieved from McGill Student Law Association: McGill University: http://www.lsa.mcgill.ca/pubdocs/files/sentencingincanadi anlaw/383-schurman_sentencingincanadianlaw_Winter2008.doc

Christie, N. (. (1986). The Ideal Victim. In E. A. Fattah, *From Crime Policy to Victim Policy.* New York: St. Martin's Press.

Criminal Code of Canada. (2014, May 4). *233. Infanticide .* Retrieved from Your Law: On Canadian Law: http://yourlaws.ca/criminal-code-canada/233-infanticide

Davetian, B. (2009). Chapter 9: Towards a Cultural Sociology of Civility. In B. Davetian, *Civility: A Cultural History eBook* (pp. 1-115). Toronto: University of Toronto Press.

Davis, A. (2004). Co-authoring identity: Digital storytelling in an urban middle school . *THEN Journal,* http://thenjournal.org/feature/61/.

Ellis, C. (2007). Telling Secrets, Revealing Lives: Relational Ethics in Research With Intimate Others. *Qualitative Inquiry*, 3-29.

Ellis, C. A. (2011). Autoethnography: An Overview. *Forum: Qualitative Social Research. 12:1,*, 1-18.

Englander, M. (2012). The Interview: Data Collection in Descriptive Phenomenological Human Scientific Research. *Journal of Phenomenological Psychology. Jan2012, Vol. 43 Issue 1,* 13-35.

Etherington, K. (2004). Chapter One: Introduction. In K. Etherington, *Becoming a Reflexive Researcher: Travellers'Tales* (pp. 16-26). London: Jessica Kingsley Publishers.

Etherington, K. (2004). Chapter Ten: Autoethnography. In K. Etherington, *Becoming a Reflexive Practioner: Travellers; Tales* (pp. 137-149). London: Jessica Kingsley Publishers.

Etherington, K. (2004). Chapter Two - Reflexivity: Meanings and Other Matters. In K. Etherington, *Becoming a Reflexive Researcher:* (pp. 27-39). London: Jessica Kingsley Publisher.

Feldman, R. (2012). Parent-Infant Synchrony: A biobehavioral model of mutual influences in the formation of affiliative bonds. *Monographs of the Society for Research in Child Development, Vol. 77 Issue 2,* 42-51.

Finkelhor, D. (2008). *Childhood Victimization: Violence, crime and abuse in the lives of young people.* New York: Oxford.

Finkelhor, D. (2008). Developmental Victimology: The Comprehensive Study of Childhood Victimizations. In D. Finkelhor, *Childhood Victimization: Violence, Crime, and Abuse in the Lives of Young People* (pp. 9-32). New York: Oxford University Press.

Fitzroy, L. (2001). Violent women: questions for feminist theory, practice and policy. *Critical Social Policy, 21(1), 7.*, 7-34.

Fitzroy, L. L. (1999). II. Mother/daughter incest: Making sense of the unthinkable. . *Feminism And Psychology, 9(4)*, 402-405. doi:10.1177/0959353599009004004.

Fortier, M. A., DiLillo, D., Messman-Moore, T. L., Peugh, J., DeNardi, K. A., & and Gaffey, K. J. (2009). Severity of Child Sexual Abuse and Revictimization: The Mediating Role of Coping and Trauma Sumptoms. *Faculty Publications, Department of Psychology* , Paper 400.

Fox, H. B. (2001). *The Healing Way of Beauty.* Delhi: Indian Board of Alternative Medicines.

Fox, H. B. (2012). *A Body of Evidence.* Regina: HealthPress.

Fox, H. B. (2014). *The Write to Justice.* Regina: LifeWrite & HBFox.

Fox, H. B. (2014, April 26). *The Write to Justice - Youtube video.* Retrieved from YouTube: https://www.youtube.com/watch?v=VHtLjummW5U&no redirect=1

Frank, A. W. (2013). *The Wounded Storyteller: Body, Illness and Ethics, Second Edition*. Chicago: University of Chicago Press.

Frey, J. (2003). *A Million Little Pieces*. New York: Doubleday.

Gilmore, L. (2001). *The Limits of Autobiography: Trauma and Testimony*. Ithaca: Cornwall University Press.

Goldberg, S. (2011). *Problem Solving in Canada's Courtrooms: A guide to therapeutic justice*. Ottawa: National Judicial Institute.

Goldenberg, I., & Goldenberg, H. (2013). Family Therapy: Narrative Therapy. In R. Corsini, & D. Wedding, *Current Psychotherapies 8th Edition* (pp. 413-416). Toronto: Nelson Education.

Government of Canada. (2001). *Assisted Human Reproduction Act (S.C. 2004, c. 2)*. Retrieved July 6, 2014, from Justice Laws Website: http://laws-lois.justice.gc.ca/eng/acts/A-13.4/

Government of Ontario. (2013, October 27). *Criminal Injuries Compensation Board*. Retrieved from Criminal Injuries Compensation Board: http://www.cicb.gov.on.ca/en/

Greaves, J. C. (2013). Sex-selective Abortion in the US: Does Roe v. Wade Protect Arbitrary Gender Discrimination. *Civil Rights Law Journal Vol. 23:3*, 333-363.

Griffin, A., & May, V. (2012). Narrative Analysis and Interpretative Phenomenological Analysis. In C. Seale, *Researching Society*

and Culture 3rd ed. (pp. 441 - 458). London: SAGE
Publications Ltd.

Hansen, J. (2013, March 29). *Continental Feminism.* Retrieved from
Stanford Encyclopedia of Philosophy:
http://plato.stanford.edu/entries/femapproach-
continental/

Held, L. R. (2012). CAN'T A MOTHER SING THE BLUES?
Postpartum Depression and the Construction of
Motherhood in Late 20th-Century America. *History of
Psychology Vol. 15, No. 2,* 107–123.

Hill, J. (2009). *Working with Victims of Crime: A manual applying research
to clinical practice.* Ottawa: Ministry of Justice Canada.

Hoijer, B. (2004, June 17). The discourse of global compassion: the
audience and media reporting of human suffering. *Media,
Culture and Society,* p. 19.

Hunt, C. (1998). Autobiography and the Psychotherapeutic Process.
In C. Hunt, & F. Sampson, *The Self on the Page" Theory and
practice of creative writing in personal development* (pp. 181-197).
London: Jessica Kingsley Publishers.

Hunt, C. (2004). Reading Ourselves: Imagining the Reader in the
Writing Process. In G. H. Edited by Bolton, *The Writing
Cure: An Introductory Handbook of Writing in Counselling and
Therapy* (pp. 35-43). London: Brunner/Rougledge.

Janov, A. (2006). *Primal Healing.* Pompton Plains: New Page Books.

Janov, A. (2007). *Primal Healing.* Franklin Lakes: The Career Press.

Janov, A., & Holden, E. M. (1975). *Primal Man: The new consciousness.* New York: Crowell.

Johns Hopkins Medicine. (2013, September 7). *Anatomy of the Brain.* Retrieved from Johns Hopkins Medicine Health Library: http://www.hopkinsmedicine.org/healthlibrary/conditions /nervous_system_disorders/anatomy_of_the_brain_85,P00 773/

Karmen, A. (2006, 2010). *Crime Victims: An Introduction to Victimology.* Belmont: Wadsworth, Cengage Learning.

Lambert, J. (Director). (2013). *Center for Digital Storytelling History* [Motion Picture].

Langer, R. (2012). 'Mother of Sorrows': Post-Partum Mental Disorder and the Law across Five Jurisdictions. *Psychiatry, Psychology and Law, Vol. 19, No. 3,* 358–388.

MacIntosh, S. C. (2004). *The Links Between Animal Abuse and Family Violence, as Reported by Women Entering Shelters in Calgary Communities.* Cremona, Alberta: RESOLVE Alberta.

Margolin G., G. E. (2000). The effects of family and community violence on children. *Annual Review of Psychology, Volume 51,* 445-79.

Markestyn, T. (1992). *The Psychological Impact of Nonsexual Criminal Offenses on Victims*. Retrieved from Ministry of the Solicitor General of Canada. : http://ww2.ps-sp.gc.ca/publications/corrections/199221_e.asp

Martin, C. G. (2013). The Role of Cumulative Trauma, Betrayal, and Appraisals in Understanding Trauma Symptomatology. *Psychological Trauma: Theory, Research, Practice, and Policy Vol. 5 No. 2*, 110–118.

Maynes, M. J., Pierce, J. L., & Laslett, B. (2012). *Telling Stories: The Use of Personal Narratives in the Social Sciences and History: Kindle Edition*. Ithaca: Cornell University Press.

Meisenchaum, D. (2006). *Understanding Reslience in Children and Adults: Implications for Prevention and Interventions*. Waterloo: University of Waterloo.

Millers, W. R. (1999). Chapter 1 - Spirituality and Health. In W. R. Miller, *Integrating spirituality into treatment: Resources for* (pp. 1-16). Albuquerque: University of New Mexico.

Murphy, M. (2012). How Our Rallying Cry Got Co-Opted and Why We Need to Take it Back. *Herizons* , 20 - 23.

Nussbaum, M. C. (2001). *Upheavals of Thought: The Intelligence of Emotions (Kindle Edition)*. New York: Cambridge University Press.

Ontario Ombudsman. (2007). *Adding Insult to Injury: Investigation into the Treatment of Victims by the Criminal Injuries Compensation Board*. Ottawa: Office of the Ontario Ombudsman.

Oprah.com. (2006, January 26). *Oprah's Questions for James*. Retrieved from Oprah.com: http://www.oprah.com/oprahshow/Oprahs-Questions-for-James

Pearson, P. (1997). *When she was bad*. New York: Penguin.

Pearson, P. (2014). *Opening Heaven's Door - What the dying may be trying to tell us about where they're going*. Toronto: Random House Canada.

Pennebaker, J. (1997 Revised). *Opening up : the healing power of expressing emotions*. New York: Guilford Press.

Pennebaker, J. W. (1990). The Downside of Writing. In J. W. Pennebaker, *Opening Up: The Healing Power of Confiding in Others* (pp. 202-206). New York: William Morrow and Company.

Pennebaker, J. W. (1995). *Emotion, Discloaure and Health*. Washington, D.C.: American Psychological Association.

Pennebaker, J. W. (1995). *Emotion, Disclosure, and Health*. Washington D.C. : American Psychological Association.

Perreault, S. J. (2004). *Multiple Victimization in Canada*. Ottawa: Canadian Centre for Justice Statistics.

Perry, B., & Szalavitz, M. (2007). *The Boy Who Was Raised as a Dog: And Other Stories from a Child Psychiatrist's Notebook--What Traumatized Children Can Teach Us About* . Basic Books, Kindle Edition.

Repko, A. F. (2011). Chapter One: Defining Interdisciplinary Studies. . In A. F. Repko, *Interdisciplinary Research, Process and Theory* (pp. 3-31). Thousand Oaks, California: SAGE.

Rivas, C. (2013). Writing a Research Report. In C. Seale, *Researching Society and Culture 3rd Edition* (pp. 497-517). London: Sage Publications.

Roach, K. (1999). *Due Process and Victims' Rights: The New Law and Politics of Criminal Justice*. Toronto: University of Toronto Press.

Roberts, J. V., & Erez, E. (2004). Communication in Sentencing: Exploring the Expressive Function of Victim Impact Statements. *International Review of Victimology Vol. 10*, 223-244.

Rosenberg, J. W. (2006). *The Importance of Fathers in the Healthy Development of Children*. Office on Child Abuse and Neglect., U.S. Children's Bureau.

Russell, S. &. (2002). Re-membering: responding to commonly asked questions. *The International Journal of Narrative Therapy and Community Work, No. 2*, 45-61.

Schaeffer, J.-M. (2013, March 8). *Fictional vs. Factual Narration.* Retrieved from The Living Book of Narratology - The University of Hamburg: http://wikis.sub.uni-hamburg.de/lhn/index.php/Fictional_vs._Factual_Narratio n

Seidman, I. (1998). *Interviewing as Qualitative Research: A Guide for Researchers in Education and the Social Sciences., 3rd ed.* New York: Teachers College Press.

Shaw, M., & Dubois, S. (1995). *Understanding Violence By Women: A Review of the Literature: Introduction.* Ottawa: Correctional Service Canada.

Sherwin, R. K. (1994). Law Frames: Historical Truth and Narrative Necessity in a Criminal Case. *Standford Law Review*, 39-83.

Statistics Canada. (2005). *Female Offenders in Canada.* Ottawa: Government of Canada.

Statistics Canada. (2010, Summer). *Violent Victimization.* Retrieved from Criminal victimization in Canada, 2009: http://www.statcan.gc.ca/pub/85-002-x/2010002/article/11340-eng.htm

Stop It With Me. (2013, November 15). *Child Abuse Story*. Retrieved
from YouTube Video
http://www.youtube.com/watch?v=T8bUj-EzuwA

The New York Times. (2006, January 27). *Author Is Kicked Out of
Oprah Winfrey's Book Club*. Retrieved from The New York
Times:
http://www.nytimes.com/2006/01/27/books/27oprah.ht
ml?_r=0

Toronto Star. (accessed 2014). Toronto Star Archives. *Toronto Star*.

Tutu, D. M. (2000). *No Future Without Forgiveness*. Bournemouth:
Image Publishing.

Tutu, D., & Tutu, M. (2014). *The Book of Forgiving: The Fourfold Path
for Healing Ourselves and Our World*. Vancouver:
HarperCollins. Kindle Edition.

United Nations General Assembly. (1985, November 29).
*Declaration of Basic Principles of Justice for Victims of Crime and
Abuses of Power*. Retrieved from United Nations General
Assembly:
http://www.un.org/documents/ga/res/40/a40r034.htm

University of California - Irvine. (2005, August 18). *Neuroscientists
Identify How Trauma Triggers Long-Lasting Memories In The
Brain*. Retrieved from Science Daily:

http://www.sciencedaily.com/releases/2005/08/05081417 5315.htm

unknown. (1980, March 10). Postbirth Blues. *Time. 115*, p. 58.

Walker, L. (2009, June). *The Battered Woman Syndrome, Third Edition (FOCUS ON WOMEN)*. New York: Springer Publishing Co., Inc. Retrieved from http://www2.webster.edu/~woolflm/walker2.html

Wemmers, J. (2008). Victim Participation and Therapeutic Jurisprudence. *Victims and Offenders, 3*, 165-191.

Wexler, D. B. (2008). Two Decades of Therapeutic Jurisprudence. *Touro Law Review Vol. 24 Issue 1*, 17-29.

White, M. (1994, May). Naming Abuse and Breaking from its Effects. (C. McLean, Interviewer)

Zaki, J. &. (2012). The neuroscience of empathy: progress, pitfalls and promise. *Nature neuroscience vol 15 | number 5* , 675-680.